Anne,

Thanks for swinging by and enjoy the

Long Road Back to Las Vegas

book!

Cheers, Alan

7-13-19

Long Road Back to Las Vegas

How Las Vegas and the Golden Knights
Healed a Journalist's Wounds

ALAN SNEL

Long Road Back to Las Vegas
How Las Vegas and the Golden Knights Healed a Journalist's Wounds

LVSPORTSBIZ.com
Las Vegas, NV 89135

ISBN: 978-1-949720-09-9

Printed in the United States
10 9 8 7 6 5 4 3 2 1

For more information or to contact the author, please go to
www.LVSportsBiz.com
asnel@LVSportsBiz.com

Cover Design by: Mark Antonuccio

In memory of Harriet Snel

She left us five years ago in August 2013. But I still feel my mother's presence and she's helping me now.

"The road is hard. Alan Snel is harder."

-- Jeff Houck

Foreword

Alan Snel had lots of reasons to be angry with the world.

He was pedaling his beloved road bike when a distracted car driver slammed him from behind. Alan was knocked unconscious. He woke in a hospital with two broken bones in his spine. He had suffered a severe concussion. A hideous bruise spanned his leg. His knee swelled to nearly the size of his head.

The driver who plowed into Alan did not call for help or offer help.

Incredibly, the driver was not even ticketed by police.

Alan's injuries were so severe that he could not work. He could not afford his medical bills.

When I prepared to see Alan at his home in Florida, I considered bringing an Old Testament to remind him of the Book of Job. Like the famous sufferer in the Bible, Alan had withstood weeks of misery with sores all over his body. I worried that Alan, like Job, was about to be threatened by a sea monster.

When we met in his house, Alan wore a neck brace and labored to walk with unsteady steps. He couldn't drive or shop for groceries. He struggled to get in and out of chairs.

Alan had only two requests for me.

He asked for Chinese food, and he asked for fresh fruit. That was all. I could hardly believe it. He did not seem to possess an ounce of self-pity.

Though Alan's body was crushed, his spirit remained strong. He easily could have dwelled on everything that had gone wrong. Instead, he remained focused on what he could still do better.

He was full of hope. He had taken some of the worst that life could throw at him, and, miraculously, he was still alive. So was his 17-year-old dog, Pugsy, who waddled and wheezed and made Alan smile.

The whole horrible bike accident had led Alan to take an unvarnished look at his life. What did he really enjoy? What could he do without? (Unfortunately, there was no way he was giving up his irrational love of the Mets.) He was 55 years old. He was determined to launch a fresh start. He was plowing ahead and not looking back.

A few months later, he had moved himself across the country and launched a fledgling business that, like Alan, did not know the meaning of the word quit. It became the premier website for sports business news in one of the nation's fastest-growing markets.

In hindsight, I realized that Alan had done me a terrific favor. In exchange for some egg rolls, chicken lo mein, and grapefruit, Alan had served up something far more valuable -- inspiration. If you've ever felt beaten down, or sorry for yourself, or at a key crossroads with no obvious path forward, then read the story of Alan Snel and fill yourself with motivation.

He'll teach you about work. He'll teach you about life. Most of all, though, he'll teach you one unforgettable lesson: Wear the damn bike helmet.

-- Mark Obmascik
Denver, Colorado

Introduction

On the morning of March 7, 2017, I set out for a bike ride from my house in Vero Beach, Fla. It was supposed to be a three-hour, 40-mile round trip to Fort Pierce and back.

It turned out the bike ride took me all the way back to Las Vegas.

This book is about that emotional and physical passage, about how a distracted motorist who probably was in no condition to operate a motorized vehicle slammed his car into me from behind, knocked me out cold and set events into motion that would lead me back to Las Vegas.

Don't be fooled by all the talk in this book of bicycling and launching a news website in Las Vegas that covered the expanding sports industry in a dynamic market in the desert. There are a lot of words about the launch of the NHL Vegas Golden Knights and the team's miracle season that galvanized a hurting community.

At its essence, this book is about recovering from a physical trauma, finding a new purpose in order to move forward and realizing a goal through sheer persistence. My hope is people will read this book and it will help them through some tough times, whatever their trauma may be. Recovery is never done alone. And writing a book draws help from all people, too. I have much gratitude for my sister, Deborah Snel Kalra, who read an early draft of this book and offered insightful suggestions on writing about trauma.

Talented photographer Daniel Clark, whose work for LVSportsBiz.com was spectacular during the 2018 Stanley Cup Final, took the main photo of my cracked bicycle helmet that appears on the book cover. Clark's splendid photos are also featured in this book. He lives in metro Las Vegas in Henderson.

Many thanks to gifted graphics designer and hiker Mark Antonuccio, a Las Vegas friend who created the book's front and back covers. Adding literary tips and much-needed writing recommendations were two old crafty newspaper buddies -- former Palm Beach Post investigative reporter and ex-central New York state journalist Gary Kane, of New York, and former Palm Beach Post Treasure Coast editor and columnist Glenn Henderson, of Fort Pierce, Fla.

Another old newspaper colleague, former Denver Post environmental writer and noted author Mark Obmascik, wrote such a good foreword that I wished he wrote this whole book. And many thanks to Cassandra Cousineau, a Las Vegas writer who suggested the publisher for this book and continues to contribute terrific stories for LVSports-Biz.com. This book was a collective effort. And writing it was a journey I will always remember just like any long and satisfying bicycle ride.

1

It was another typical muggy Florida morning and I was pedaling along two-lane Old Dixie Highway, a sleepy road north of Fort Pierce in early March 2017. I was on a quiet stretch of a daily 40-mile bike ride through a small intracoastal town called St. Lucie Village, a leafy community of 600 people on the north side of Fort Pierce harbor, about 2½ hours north of Miami on Florida's east coast.

And then out of nowhere came another typical Florida scene -- I was bouncing off a car windshield and left unresponsive, my bicycle reduced to a twisted metal pretzel by a distracted motorist at 8:03 a.m. March 7.

A driver named Dennis Brophy, 64 at the time, nearly killed me when he slammed his 2016 white Chevrolet Cruze into me from behind as I rode my 20-pound Cannondale road bicycle. He did not even try to drive around me. He didn't even brake.

On the Florida traffic crash report filled out by St. Lucie County sheriff's deputy G. Felix, Brophy listed his address as 709 South 5th Street in Fort Pierce -- a mental health center that works with substance abuse patients. I found out later he worked as a counselor there.

I know that stretch of Old Dixie Highway well from my daily bicycle rides. Motorists routinely travel at 40 to 55 mph in that area. Let's be conservative and say Brophy was moving at 40 mph -- that's still a violent collision with a bicyclist moving at 15 mph. Sadly, many bicyclists have been killed in Florida from less violent collisions caused by people driving cars.

I was lucky. I initially was knocked out, unresponsive. But I eventually came to and I was alive.

A witness driving a car in the opposite direction, James Pedra, of Fort Pierce, said Brophy crashed his car into me from behind, "causing the rider to roll up on the hood and make contact with the windshield," according to the crash report. A towing company called Auto Reserve removed Brophy's vehicle. The deputy took my crushed bicycle to the sheriff's office evidence center.

The witness, Pedra, said in the report, "The car made no apparent attempt to pass the bicyclist crashing into the rear of the bicycle."

Brophy said he never saw me even though I was biking in the proper position in the lane in front of him. Brophy told the deputy he was blinded by a bright light and "never saw the bicyclist until he hit him." Brophy was driving south. The bright light -- the sun -- was to the east. The crash report also said Brophy was "inattentive," according to the report's "Driver Distracted By" box.

There's more -- and here's the part where Brophy admitted he was distracted and drowsy. "Fatigue/asleep" were cited in the crash report's "Driver's Condition at Time of Crash" box.

Brophy said he was "in the process of inhaling a breathing treatment" -- not 100 percent focused on the road -- and that he suffered from extreme sleep apnea. Brophy noted he "has yet to participate in a sleep study or use a C-pap machine," the crash report said.

Brophy caused the crash. I was described as a "non-motorist" in the crash report. I committed, "No improper action," the report said.

But the St. Lucie County sheriff's office did not issue a ticket to Brophy for his negligent driving or for failing to pass me by the required distance of three feet, which is a law in Florida.

I don't recall Brophy smashing his car into me. All this information is documented in the crash report.

Felix, the responding St. Lucie County deputy, called my emergency contact, who was my sister, Deborah Kalra in the Baltimore area. My sister knows I ride my bicycle every morning. She also knows that Florida is notorious for being the state in the country with the most bicyclists killed.

So, every morning at her job, she keeps her cell phone in plain sight. How sad is this? My sister has her phone handy because of Florida's notorious track record of motorists driving their cars into bicyclists. On this morning, a little after 8 a.m., the call came to her. The one she never wanted to receive. But had prepared for.

"This is Deputy Felix, are you Deborah Kalra?"

My sister said yes. And before the deputy even told her, she knew that he was calling to inform her that I was struck while bicycling by a motorist. "What's his condition,?" she asked the deputy.

A thousand miles away, my first conscious memory was waking up at Lawnwood Medical Center in Fort Pierce, Florida later that morning. An EMT was wheeling me through a hospital hallway. He leaned down to me and whispered in a matter-of-fact tone, "You were hit by a car."

2

I suffered two broken vertebra and the fracture of one of them nearly killed me. One was in my neck. The C2. The other was in my lower back. The L1. I would later learn from a doctor treating me that the breaks were not facing my spinal column, which meant I could move.

The disc fracture in my neck was a fraction of an inch from causing death or paralysis. Another sister in South Florida, Leiba Bonnardel, who was alerted by Deborah to go to the hospital in Fort Pierce, came to see me at the Lawnwood Medical Center ICU. She said the doctor told her that if the break in the donut -- the disc -- was just a fraction over, it could have meant that I would have been paralyzed or killed.

Doctors initially said they were not going to move me until it was determined whether I was paralyzed or not, Leiba said. "It was a sheer miracle. The doctors said you were so close to being paralyzed from the neck down," Leiba said.

Oh, there were a few other things. I also had a bad concussion. And the blow to my body from Brophy's car was so severe that bruising ran up and down the side of my right leg. So much blood and fluid had collected on my right knee that it was the size of a soccer ball.

My mother, Harriet Snel, died in August 2013 and I believe a guardian angel with strong connections to my mom was watching over me that morning. The violent force of Brophy's car slamming into my bicycle and myself could have easily killed me. To this day, when I reflect back -- and I consciously try not to look back too often -- I wonder why I was spared when other bicyclists are killed around Florida and our country every year.

When I recovered the crushed bicycle and the helmet at the sheriff's evidence facility, I also saw what happened to my helmet.

It was cracked and it had saved me from a much worse traumatic brain injury. The helmet saved me from death or being a vegetable. The helmet is on the cover of this book.

I stayed overnight in the hospital. What I remember is the bright light of the ICU room practically blinding me as I tried to sleep overnight. It was a horrible night. I dozed off from the sheer exhaustion of the trauma, only to wake up on the hour with that bright light shining in my face.

By late Wednesday afternoon the next day, a doctor came into my room, fitted me with a big neck brace, advised me to keep it on 24/7 for the rest of the month of March and sent me home to Vero Beach, about 15 miles to the north.

Leiba, my sister from North Miami Beach, and my father from Boca Raton drove me back to my house I had bought just more than a year earlier. That night, I rested on my back with the neck brace keeping my head in place on my bed and thought to myself, "What the hell am I doing in Vero Beach?'

The helmet on the cover of this book.

My Ravaged Bicycle parts recovered from the scene

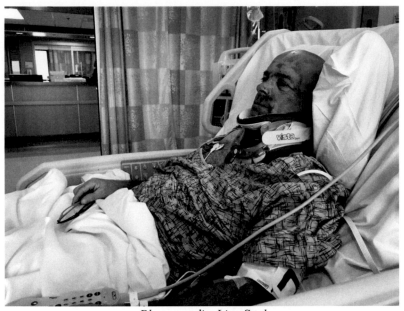

Photo credit: Lisa Snel

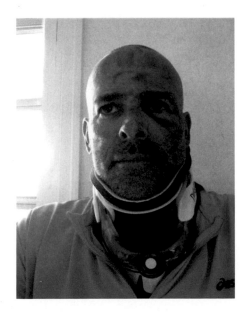

3

Right about now, you might be asking yourself what was I doing bicycling on a quiet road south of Vero Beach heading into Fort Pierce?

Riding my bicycle in the mornings is a daily ritual. It's my coffee that gets my day off to a start and offers time for meditation, reflection and a review of the daily stuff I hope to deal with during the rest of the day.

On the morning of March 7, 2017, I was making a living as a freelance writer while living in Vero Beach, a quiet Florida city that was actually two cities in one -- the elite, rich barrier island on the Atlantic Ocean and the middle class part back on the mainland where I lived about a mile west of U.S. 1, not too far from the old Dodgertown spring training center. It's a famous former baseball spring camp, where the Dodgers used to spend the month of March every year before the Major League Baseball club moved to Arizona.

In fact, only the day before, on Monday March 6, I joined a pal who worked at the Palm Beach Post in West Palm Beach for a Houston Astros spring training game at a new spring training ballpark in West Palm Beach. I took photos at the ballpark for a freelance story I wrote on the business of spring training complexes in Florida for a Florida politics website.

It turned out that was the last story I wrote in Florida. I had moved to Vero Beach about a year earlier from a newspaper job in Las Vegas, where I covered the business side of sports and stadiums for the Las Vegas Review-Journal. That was my newspaper specialty -- reporting on the intersection of sports, stadiums, business and politics.

I first covered the topic for the Denver Post, where I covered Denver City Hall about 20 years earlier. I covered the Denver Broncos' attempt at getting public money -- sales tax revenue collected in a six-county area that included Denver. As a metro newspaper reporter, I was fascinated that a private person -- like former Denver Broncos owner Pat Bowlen -- could walk into the Colorado state capitol and ask for free money to help build a football stadium for his NFL team.

I covered the Broncos stadium subsidy debate in Denver. And it launched me into a satisfying new chapter of my newspaper career -- covering the business side of stadiums and sports in several big metropolitan areas that included South Florida, Seattle and Tampa Bay. Along the way, I even launched a new sports-business website for FOX Sports called FoxSportsBiz.com.

So, in late 2012, I moved to Las Vegas to cover this dynamic sports-business beat for the local daily newspaper. Las Vegas was a great place to cover that beat, especially because there was a constant flow of stadium and arena proposals to write about.

But when a secret buyer purchased the Review-Journal in late 2015, it set off a string of events that led me to eventually find a new reporting job in Vero Beach of all places.

In December 2015, the Review-Journal staff was assembled and informed a secret investor had purchased the newspaper. I wondered right then if the secret buyer knew the mission of a newspaper: to purvey complete, truthful information and serve as the vanguard for the First Amendment. If the new owner wanted to keep his identity secret, maybe he might not be the right person to buy a newspaper.

Well, the Review-Journal's reporters made lots of national headlines and won lots of journalism awards for unmasking the secret owner -- none other than local Las Vegas billionaire casino tycoon Sheldon Adelson, who bought the Review-Journal for way more than what it was valued.

Adelson installed a new publisher and a new executive editor, ushering in a new era at the Review-Journal (after the PR mess of his initial secret identity.)

Adelson, CEO of Las Vegas Sands Corp., was also involved in trying to get $750 million in public money to help build a new Raiders football stadium in Las Vegas and lure the NFL team from Oakland. And guess who would be covering that public policy discussion on that topic for Adelson's newspaper in Las Vegas? I'm a newspaper veteran of covering debates on using public money to help pay for sports stadiums and arenas.

In every market where I covered this policy debate, there were always heated political discussions about the extent to which investing public dollars in stadiums benefited the local community. The notion of giving hundreds of millions of dollars to wealthy team owners is an old topic, but remains a controversial one. It required in-depth, hard-hitting news reporting to look at the pros and cons of giving corporate welfare to the wealthiest members of a local town -- namely, professional major-league team owners.

In January 2016, I reported and wrote a story for Adelson's Review-Journal outlining the issue of using public dollars to help pay for a stadium. It was a professional newspaper story -- one that I have reported for other metro newspapers. I didn't see anything in the story that seemed unusually inflammatory, based on covering this same topic in previous metro markets.

But Adelson's new executive editor at the time, Craig Moon, did not allow the story to be published in the Review-Journal. Only after I removed some comments that opposed the stadium did the news story run. This is not the journalism I had practiced at previous metro newspapers. My stadium story was held and would only run if comments that were unfavorable to Adelson's stadium project were removed.

In response, I made a decision. A month later in early 2016, I was in Vero Beach interviewing for a news writing job for a weekly newspaper called Vero Beach 32963.

4

Yes, I was back in Florida in early 2016. Know the place well. I worked for the Palm Beach Post and South Florida Sun-Sentinel in the 1990s and the Florida Today daily newspaper in Melbourne, Fla. and Tampa Tribune in the early 2000s. I recall Vero Beach from my days of living in Jensen Beach in Martin County when I worked for the Palm Beach Post in the mid-1990s and did bicycle rides north of about 30 miles to Vero.

For a small city, Vero Beach had an active bicyclist community because bicyclists enjoyed pedaling along the scenic oceanfront A1A both north and south of Vero Beach that had much less car traffic than the busy roads of South Florida.

The oceanside residential communities of Vero Beach were filled with information-hungry retirees, who enjoyed reading a weekly publication called Vero Beach 32963. The newspaper owner was Milton Benjamin, a former Washington Post executive and editor who had lived in Vero Beach for more than 30 years. Benjamin's news staff included veteran reporters and writers who produced in-depth local copy for the locals on the barrier island. In February 2016, I accepted an offer to report business news for Vero Beach 32963.

I also purchased a cozy ranch house on the mainland in Vero Beach, hoping my sister in North Miami Beach -- who is a mother of nine -- and my dad in Boca Raton would visit often so that they could use the house a family retreat and refuge from the busy, hectic conditions of South Florida.

In early March 2016, I moved into my new house. I also had the new job. And every morning I would ride my bicycle on what I thought would be quiet and safe roads north and south of Vero Beach.

But it took only a few months to realize that reporting and writing news in Vero Beach was not like the experience I had in Las Vegas. It meant I was a poor fit for Vero Beach 32963. I thrived on reporting sports-business stories on proposed stadium projects. But the only sports venue to cover was an old spring training ballpark that was now marketed as an all-purpose sports center a mile from my house. The old Dodgertown.

Most of Vero Beach 32963's stories were devoted to deep-dive stories on ultra-local community issues that did not resonate with me. I was bored, the kiss of death for any reporter at a newspaper. So, I switched gears. I returned to the bicycle world in October 2017. And my new business partner was a prominent bicycle tour operator in Las Vegas who was a terrific friend.

Good-bye newspapers. Hello bicycles.

5

Jared Fisher owned Escape Adventures, a leading bicycle touring operation based in his Las Vegas Cyclery bike shop center in the western suburbs of Las Vegas called Summerlin. A marathon mountain biker and bicycle lover, Fisher was a good friend and sort of a kindred bicycle spirit.

I was a newspaperman who loved the bicycle and all of its magical powers. The bicycle's passenger was also its engine and I loved this human-powered machine that could take you to work in busy cities or to mountain tops in quiet, natural settings or to your local ice cream shop a mile or two from your home.

In between working as a sports-business journalist for the Tampa Tribune and the Las Vegas Review-Journal, I devoted 6½ years of my life in Tampa to furthering the cause of bicycling in the Tampa Bay market.

I made a living as a bicycle activist. It was not very lucrative. But it was satisfying to see how my efforts motivated so many people who hardly rode a bicycle to take to Tampa's streets and join bike events I had organized on restaurant bike tours and rides around my Tampa neighborhood called Seminole Heights

Who knew that my nomadic newspaper life was preparing me all along to increase the profile of bicycling in the Tampa, a city where so many motorists endangered the lives of people who chose to pedal a bicycle as a means of transportation?

I quit the Tampa Tribune in mid-2006 and created a group of Tampa Bay area bicycle stores that enlisted me to politically lobby for bicyclists, stage bicycle festivals, work on bike safety projects and spread the word of the goodness of bicycling.

I even helped create an informal neighborhood bicycle club in Tampa, where I created local bike tours of slow poke non-Lycra-wearing bicyclists and held bike events like bike movie nights in my backyard. I smile when I remember people sitting in folding chairs watching the movie, Breaking Away, under the stars on a makeshift screen behind my bungalow house.

So, when my reporting life sagged in Vero Beach, I fell back on bicycling and my friend, Fisher, the bicycle man of Las Vegas who opened a 10,000-square foot bike shop that was the most environmentally friendly bicycle store in the country. That was how I met Fisher. I had just moved to Las Vegas in November 2012 and one of my first stories at the Las Vegas Review-Journal was on the new environmentally-friendly building that housed Fisher's bike store and bike-touring business.

His Las Vegas Cyclery building in suburban Summerlin, 12 miles west of the Strip, created more energy than it consumed thanks to its more than 200 solar panels and a wind turbine. Fisher and his wife, Heather, also operated a successful bike touring business called Escape Adventures. Their business' bike tours were held across the West, from the Oregon coast and the Grand Canyon to Utah and the Colorado Rockies.

Fisher was also a terrific bicycle spirit, a modest and honest man who could bike literally through the night. I realized that after I quit Vero Beach 32963, I had a mental inventory of Florida's best bicycle rides right in my head. These were my favorite bike rides around the state.

So, I took a map of Florida and highlighted these routes. They included pedaling around Lake Okeechobee on a trail in the center of the state; the Withlacoochee Trail through a forest north of Tampa; a lovely ride called the Ormond Loop along the Atlantic Coast and intracoastal north of Ormond Beach; and the rolling hills of Lake County outside Orlando. (Yes, there are hills in Florida.)

I convinced Fisher to come to Florida in October 2016 to bike these rides with me to see for himself that we could collaborate on a Florida edition of Escape Adventures. And it thrilled me that saw the natural and serene beauty of these bicycle rides, too.

Fisher and I biked eight routes all around Florida in three days from the Atlantic Ocean to mighty Lake Okeechobee in the center of the state to the Pinellas Trail on Florida's west coast in St. Petersburg. I had written newspaper travel stories on most of these bike rides and I was convinced that the landscape beauty along the routes would make it an attractive and economically feasible enterprise.

Among my favorites was Ormond Loop -- a 25-mile ride through inspiring canopied state forest lands, along the Atlantic Intracoastal and a mere few pedal rotations to the Atlantic and A1A, Florida's ocean road. There was even history along the way, too -- an 1825 sugar and rum factory on the Ormond Loop route, and the ruins are still there for all to see.

Then, there was the Lake Okeechobee Scenic Trail, a path of pavement atop an earthen berm in the center of southern Florida that offered great views of The Big Lake and waterfowl and hawks of all types to gaze at.

And one of favorite rides we would offer was the Withlacoochee Trail, a terrific 46-mile ribbon of pavement that is the longest rails-to-trails path in Florida. All types of bicyclists, from road bicycle racers to recumbent users, used the Withlacoochee Trail. It was a summer bicycle haven because of its leafy tunnel effect. It's about an hour north of Tampa, and an hour west of Orlando, so it would be central to many Florida visitors.

To promote the Florida bike tours, Fisher used footage filmed from a drone during our bike rides and he pieced together a magnificent two-minute video that any Florida tourism agency would have been proud to show. It was game on for Escape Adventures Florida.

The Escape Adventures Florida vehicle.   Photo credit: Jeff Houck

I flew to Las Vegas in early November 2016. Fisher gave me the keys to an Escape Adventures minivan wrapped in Escape Adventures branding. And we loaded 13 bicycles of all sizes inside and outside the Honda Odyssey for my drive back. It was our bike tour fleet and the bikes were ideal for our tours. They had the performance level of a road bike, while also having wider tires that would provide our bike riders and tour customers with a stable ride. The wider tires would also allow me to lead bike tours on dirt roads, such as Jungle Trail, a lovely road amid leafy trees and under a tree-limb canopy along the Intracoastal north of Vero Beach.

For the second time in nine months, I drove across the country from Las Vegas to Vero Beach. It took two days of driving non-stop, punctuated by breaks to nap, eat and use the bathroom. After I reached my home in Vero Beach, I used a spare bedroom as the designated bicycle and tour storage room. Escape Adventures Florida was open for business.

6

I could not wait to promote these day bike rides and share Florida's beautiful scenery with tourists via two wheels. The bike ride offerings were listed on the Escape Adventures website and I spent days driving around Florida to share the bike tour service information with hotel concierges, tourism agency leaders and visitor centers.

Fisher's video showcased the nicest scenery in Florida -- and it was all accessible by our bike tours. How could anyone not want to pedal on Florida's best bike trails, through natural canopies and along the ocean and intracoastal waterways?

Those bicycles were comfy. And I would personally lead tourists on the nicest bike rides Florida had to offer. I began in November 2016. And a month later in December, I attended a concierge social network event at a restaurant in Orlando and chatted with a dozen hotel concierges about the bike tours.

I offered free tours for them so that they could experience the lovely rides. They were excited. But when I called to arrange the bike rides, nobody took me up on my offers.

Even in my hometown of Vero Beach, I visited two swanky hotels on the ocean and offered free bike tours to staff along the lush, canopied dirt road of Historic Jungle Trail along the intracoastal so they could see and feel Florida in a way you could never experience it from the seat of a car. Again, no takers. It was discouraging.

The fact that all those Orlando area concierges never took me up on my offer to give them free tours was an ominous business signal. The calls for the tours that I expected from tourists never came.

Then it was January and February of 2017, the months offering some of the best weather to ride a bicycle amid Florida's best scenery. Still no business. The calls never came. On Feb. 28, 2017, Fisher called with the news that I was hoping to never hear. He could no longer financially justify Escape Adventures Florida without revenues from tours. After four months of marketing what I thought were beautiful bike rides, I had failed. Fisher pulled the plug on Escape Adventures Florida.

7

One of Fisher's Escape Adventures workers arrived in Orlando March 1, 2017, and I picked him up at the airport to take him to my house in Vero Beach. He was there to load up the bikes, stuff them back in the minivan and drive them back to the Escape Adventures headquarters at Las Vegas Cyclery.

I was not upset at Fisher. How could I blame him when I had failed to generate income from the bike tours, despite all the promotional and marketing efforts I made around the state. I was disappointed in myself. I felt I was a failure. I felt I let down Fisher. And I was upset with myself that I was so wrong about tourists wanting to feel the same bike ride experiences that brought joy to me.

So, it was time to ping-pong back to reporting and writing to make a living. With my daily newspaper experience, I had a few freelance opportunities in Florida. They included writing for Peter Schorsch's Influence Magazine and Florida Politics website. And I pitched a story to Schorsch that was in my writing and reporting sweet spot. It was a status report story on spring training baseball complexes around Florida.

There was a musical chairs of several Major League Baseball teams leaving their Florida spring training homes for greener diamonds elsewhere in the Sunshine State. For example, the Houston Astros were leaving Kissimmee for a new spring training complex in West Palm Beach in 2017. The Astros were sharing the new spring baseball digs with the Washington Nationals, a team that was leaving Melbourne in Brevard County.

Meanwhile, the New York Mets were working on renovating their spring home in Port St. Lucie in St. Lucie County.

Schorsch liked the story idea, and I went back to work in a news area that was back in my comfort zone. Reporting about the business and politics of stadiums and sports. I was proud of the story. It was a solid piece of journalism. And all I needed were photos. So, I arranged to meet an Astros' spring training lobbyist at an Astros game at the new West Palm Beach ballpark Monday, March 6, 2017.

My baseball/reporter/bicycle pal Joe Capozzi from the Palm Beach Post was going to attend, too. So, Joe and I decided to a do an off-road bike ride along some canals amid a bunch of gators about five miles west of the Astros/Nationals' new ballpark.

We met several hours before the game, and pedaled along the dirt service roads on our fat-tire bikes. We then biked to the ballpark and met the Astros' ballpark PR man, Tom McNicholas. I snapped some photos of the new ballyard and a few of McNicholas for the Influence magazine story.

Later that day when I returned home to Vero Beach, I emailed the photos to Schorsch.

It was late. And I knew in the morning the next day March 7, 2017, I would return to my daily, bread-and-butter 40-mile bike ride.

8

On March 7, 2017, it was about 7 a.m. or so when I left my house in Vero Beach for an Intracoastal bridge in Fort Pierce, where I cross the span and take A1A back to Vero Beach.

I bike along a north-south road that's about three miles west of U.S. 1 and eventually cut east to Old Dixie Highway, another north-south road that leads from Indian River County into St. Lucie County and Fort Pierce.

I was riding a fascinating bicycle that I had brought back to life. The 1994 Cannondale road bicycle had a two-tone paint job, with colors showing a deep navy blue and a deep purple, It was a bicycle given to me by my former wife in 1994 when we lived in Jensen Beach, some 23 years earlier and about 30 miles south of Vero Beach.

On a bike ride a few months earlier, I passed a garage sale in Indian River County where an old fishing guide was selling mostly fishing equipment. But he had a pile of bicycle parts that intrigued me. I bought it all for $60 -- two gorgeous high-performance bike wheels, plus brakes and gear-switching equipment.

So, I asked the mechanics at my favorite Vero Beach bike shop, Orchid Island Bikes and Kayaks, to swap out the Cannondale bike's old parts for the new modern race bike parts I scored at the sale on a side street off U.S. 1 about 10 miles north of Vero Beach.

The bike had a frame that was nearly a quarter-century old, with modern road bike parts. I added my own bike saddle and pedals. And it was a sweet ride. I wore bike shorts and a red-white-and-blue bike jersey I bought from a former friend for $80. An hour later, it would be the last time I rode that bicycle.

9

It has become so routine for people operating motorized vehicles and slamming their cars and trucks into bicyclists that some newspapers don't even report it.

Like the daily newspaper that covered St. Lucie County. The St. Lucie Tribune didn't think it was newsworthy that a distracted motorist drove his car into me, sending me to the Lawnwood Medical Center Intensive Care Unit, and that the county sheriff's office thought it was OK for the driver, Brophy, to do exactly that without being cited.

But the Tampa Bay Times, clear across the state, used a different news judgment. Reporter Sharon Wynne reported the fact that Brophy drove his car into me and wrote this:

"Deputy Bryan Beaty, spokesman for the St. Lucie County Sheriff's Office, said investigators arrived at 8:08 a.m. and found Snel 'unresponsive' but he was up walking and talking by the time ambulance arrived.

"Beaty said he did not yet have the investigators' report. 'At this point, no one has been charged or cited,' Beaty said. 'The investigation is ongoing and a full report will be available in 60 days.' "

Brophy was never charged or given a ticket for anything. He walked away scot-free. Not only was there no criminal blemish, I was told by my lawyer, J. Steele Olmstead of Tampa, that he had filed for bankruptcy the year before and he had no assets to claim to help pay for lost wages, medical expenses and pain and suffering. There would be no lawsuit.

Wynne at the Tampa Bay Times followed up with a story a month later explaining why the driver was never given a ticket. In her April 3, 2017 story she quoted Beaty, the spokesman for the St. Lucie County Sheriff's Office, as saying. "He didn't intentionally hit the bicyclist and there's no evidence that indicates he purposely set out that day to go and run over a bicyclist."

Welcome to bicycle life (and death) in Florida -- the state where you can slam your car into an unexpecting, innocent bicyclist and get away with it without a ticket. In my case, Brophy admitted to the sheriff's deputy he was distracted and fatigued when he drove his car into me from behind, yet he was not held accountable for his negligence.

Under Florida law, Brophy was obliged to pass me by a minimum space of three feet. He drove his car right into me from behind, so he violated the three-foot law. But there was not even a ticket for that from the St. Lucie Sheriff's Office.

You would think the local newspaper in St. Lucie County, the Tribune, would be reporting all this. But the paper's decision to not even write a word about is telling because it shows that bicyclists getting injured, maimed and killed without motorist accountability is so common in Florida that it didn't even register with this newspaper. Welcome to The Grim Reaper, better known as the Florida motorist, who can drive his car into a bicyclist and walk away with immunity by saying these simple words, "I didn't see the bike." To this day, Brophy never apologized.

He said he never saw me when I was plain as day on the road in front of him. The numbers show Florida is the place where more bicyclists die than any other state in the country. Through the years, I have cited federal data showing exactly that. And lo and behold, even the Wall Street Journal published a story in September 2018 reporting that Florida was the deadliest state in the U.S.

And in her story, Wynne also reported Florida's dismal record of bicyclist deaths and injuries at the hands of motorists who drive too fast, distracted and without care and alertness for bicyclists (and walkers, too.)

From her Times article, Wynne wrote: "Florida is the most hostile state in the nation to bicyclists. It has the highest rate of bicycling deaths by far, according to the Centers for Disease Control and Prevention. At 7.4 fatalities per million people in 2015, the bike death rate in the Sunshine State is almost three times the national average of 2.5."

Brophy went home March 7. His record is unblemished. Meanwhile, I took an ambulance shuttle to the Lawnwood Medical Center ICU. The deputy who called my contact, a sister in the Baltimore area, said it was uncertain what physical condition I was in. There was no information at all -- except that I was awake when the ambulance arrived and talking.

By the end of the next day, I was back home in my Vero Beach house recovering. And in a strange place -- on my back in a bed without a bicycle. I had no idea whether I would ride a bicycle again. With my concussion, my mind could not focus. I wondered if I could continue being a journalist.

10

Four days after the crash, my sister Debbie came from metro Baltimore to stay with me from March 11-17, 2017. This is what she recalled from her visit. I slept most of the day. I emerged from my room a few times to grab meals.

A large contusion from my right thigh to my knee and deep leg bruising had left blood and fluid collecting on my knee, which was still ballooned from Brophy driving his car into me. The concussion left me with short-term memory loss. I repeated questions. The question I asked myself while I rested in bed, "Would I ever ride a bicycle again?"

When Brophy drove his Chevy Cruze into me that March 2017 morning, he also drove his vehicle into a powerful force -- my family and friends who helped raise some money so I could pay the bills and buy some food and who visited to offer an emotional boost.

My sister Debbie worked behind the scenes during her visit from Baltimore to work with bicycle writer Joe "Metal Cowboy" Kurmaskie from Portland and close friend Bridget Sweeten from California to set up a You Caring fundraising link online.

The force of this collision was met by the love and generosity of my friends and family and strangers in the greater bicycle community who donated a stunning $4,000 in the first 24 hours of internet fundraising so that I had money to pay my bills and meet living expenses while the case was sorted out.

As I write this, I get choked up thinking about so many people who stepped up and gave money and shared the fundraiser link to help me through those tough recovery days. My former business editor at the Las Vegas Review-Journal, Dan Behringer, sent a get well call with uplifting messages from newsroom staffers. Even Tim Etter, the owner of my favorite craft brewery in Las Vegas, Tenaya Creek, sent me a care package packed with goodies. It included a six-pack of my favorite brown ale, Bonanza Brown; a brewery ball cap I still wear today; a Tenaya Creek iron-on patch; a shirt; and a beer coozie.

Friends from around the country penned letters sharing get well wishes. I read and re-read them often. Words matter. They lifted my morale. But I still felt physically battered and beaten up at the steering wheel hands of a motorist who didn't even receive a citation. I didn't realize it at the time, but these anger and bitterness issues would remain with me much longer than I would even know at the time.

The whole situation of nearly being killed by an uncited car driver and recovering at home was strange and disorienting and here's why: I had worked as a bicycle safety and rights activist in the Tampa Bay area from 2006-2012 and warned everyone from police to elected officials to road designers that too many bicyclists were getting struck and close to being hit by motorists every single day.

I personally helped install "ghost bikes," white-painted bicycle memorials at sites along roadways where bicyclists were killed by motorists. In Tampa, I talked with family members of bicyclists killed to offer emotional support while working on public service announcements, memorial bike rides and awareness programs that advised motorists to slow down, watch for bicyclists, be patient, pass people on bikes safely and generally treat bicyclists as people operating slow-moving vehicles.

Yet here I was in mid-March 2017, badly bruised and nursing a concussion because an inattentive motorist drove his car into me from behind. But deep inside, I was thankful to be alive. My sister, Debbie, who had traveled from Baltimore to stay with me for a week, later told me she was amazed that I wasn't complaining more about my injuries. I told her that so many bicyclists are killed and left maimed from being hit by motorists in much less violent crashes than what I endured. And here I was -- moving, breathing, talking, thinking, being alive. I knew all too well that it could have easily ended with my death.

The crash, though, did leave me with questions about my future as a journalist. In the days after I was hit, I had problems with short-term memory. And after I returned home, I found it difficult to focus -- a necessity that is needed for any job let alone being a journalist. My mind was swimming when I tried to string together words and paragraphs. It left me wondering what it would be like to try and return to my job as a journalist.

11

So the month of March in 2017 was spent hardly moving and recovering. The concussion symptoms were slowly wearing off when a friend from Denver contacted me after my sister, Debbie, had returned home to Baltimore. He was Mark Obmascik, a former colleague at the Denver Post who was an award-winning environmental news writer.

Obmascik wrote a popular 2004 book, "The Big Year," documenting a year-long competition between three guys who were trying to break the North American bird watching record. The book did so well that movie rights went to Fox for a movie that included Jack Black, Steve Martin and Owen Wilson as the three zany dudes.

He also wrote a book on his summer of fourteeners -- "Halfway to Heaven," which documented a summer of climbing all the 54 mountain peaks in Colorado that were at least 14,000 feet.

Obmascik's in-laws lived on the Vero Beach barrier island and he was among a group of cherished friends who stopped by to check in on me and see how I was doing. He asked what he could bring over. I said, "Chinese food and fruits, bananas, strawberries and grapefruits."

Later that day around lunchtime, Obmascik showed up with Chinese food and fruits in tow. We went outside in the backyard and took a seat at a table. Obmascik offered a suggestion: "You have covered the business side of sports and stadiums in Las Vegas and you have been away only a year. Why don't you just go back to Vegas and report on what you were covering before on your own website?"

I listened to his words. And it clicked. I loved the idea. At the time of Obmascik's visit, my mental skills were improving. I began feeling more comfortable focusing on issues and topics. I missed covering some of the big sports-business news items in Las Vegas like the opening of T-Mobile Arena in April 2016, the state Legislature's approval later in 2016 to give $750 million to the Raiders to build their stadium in Las Vegas and the sale of Las Vegas-based UFC for more than $4 billion to IMG.

Afterwards, I wondered why I didn't have the confidence to come up with the idea of creating my own sports-business news site myself. I still had a Rolodex packed with Las Vegas area sports-business sources and I was only a year and a month removed from reporting on the high-profile topics such as the construction of T-Mobile Arena and the financing of the football stadium.

It was bittersweet to be in Vero Beach in 2016 when the arena I wrote about in Las Vegas had opened and the football stadium concept that drew so much of my Las Vegas Review-Journal attention received state approval for public funding. I was not there to report on that news.

And it stung. But who was stopping me from returning to Las Vegas and creating my own news website to report on the business of sports and stadiums. Few reporters around the country had my level of expertise and experience in this news coverage area. And what was keeping me in Vero Beach?

A news reporting job proved unsatisfying. A bicycle touring business initiative failed. A guy drove his car into me without getting a ticket. Yet, I survived the horrific crash. I had a second chance. A second lease on life. The next day, I was on the phone with a real estate agent. I was selling my house and returning to Las Vegas. The recovery from this trauma was starting.

Months later, I learned an important lesson -- out of trauma comes clarity. The idea to create a news website covering the business surrounding Las Vegas' booming sports events, new teams, stadium construction and economic development was born out of a crushed bicycle, a cracked bicycle helmet, two broken vertebra, a bad concussion and a badly beat-up leg.

When I gathered all my mental marbles, all had crystallized -- good-bye Florida, hello Las Vegas (again.)

12

One of my old sources in Las Vegas was Joe Maloof, who, with his brothers, had owned the Houston Rockets and Sacramento Kings of the National Basketball Association and was a founding partner of a new National Hockey League team in Las Vegas.

When I was at the Review-Journal, I profiled Maloof and his brother, Gavin, for a story on the guys behind the movement to create an NHL team in Las Vegas. They, along with two other brothers, George and Phil, had teamed up with mortgage insurance billionaire Bill Foley to launch a season ticket deposit campaign to show the NHL that Las Vegas was worthy of a big league hockey franchise.

A lot of team owners are stiffs. But Joe Maloof was a fun, carefree dude who once looked out his window in Huntington Beach, Calif., saw skateboarders pulling tricks on the boards and decided to stage a skateboard championship series called the Maloof Money Cup for both amateurs and pros in 2008.

I thought I'd bounce the idea of launching a sports-business website catering to reporting on Las Vegas' booming sports industry off Joe Maloof.

Vegas Golden Knights founding partner Joe Maloof.
Photo credit: Erik John Ricardo

His phone number was still in my cell phone.

We talked and he liked the idea.

In fact, he even backed the idea of buying advertising on the website.

And he recommended I call his sports marketing consultant, Kevin Kaplan.

I remember dialing Kaplan's number and walking out of my Vero Beach house to stroll on the front lawn near a maple tree.

A lot of sports marketing types are fast-talking operators, but Kaplan was easy to talk with and a straight shooter.

I bounced a name for the website off him.

"What do you think of LasVegasSportsBiz.com," I asked.

Kaplan said it was too long.

"What about LVSportsBiz.com,?" I followed up.

Kaplan said yes, that will work.

So, that was solved. I had a name for my news website.

LVSportsBiz.com

13

By April 2017, my house was up for sale and I was committed to bouncing back to Las Vegas.

But the balloon of skin around my knee needed to be drained. I was lucky. There was no structural damage to the right knee joint. But so much blood and fluid had collected in the knee that it was impeding the joint from working smoothly. It was time to drain that knee.

I drove over to my doctor about five miles north on U.S. 1 and pulled into the modern-looking medical building in quiet Indian River County. The doctor plunged a giant needle below my kneecap and the red liquid filled a mega-sized syringe. He then squirted out my blood into a beaker and repeated the process two more times. The knee joint was pivoting without a bunch of blood and fluid sloshing around in there. There would be so much fluid and blood on the knee in the coming weeks that I had to return at least two more times.

And then later in April 2017, I did my own big return. The first time I returned to the bicycle was when I rode my fat-tire bike in my backyard. I figured that if I fell, I would fall on grass and not rock-hard pavement. I was nervous and didn't tell anyone I was going to see what it was like to ride a bicycle again.

Riding a bicycle is so much of who I am. It's a big part of my identity. I was afraid to find out if this crash was going to steal that identity away from me. But I knew part of the emotional recovery meant that I had to confront this moment and see whether I would be able to pedal a bicycle again. The legs churned and they were creaky. But the body was working. It was only a few feet of pedaling.

I needed to try and return the world back to its normal self prior to the motorist striking me while I bicycled that day. And by early May, I was cycling slowly on my road bicycle. It was an astonishing feeling. It was literally like I was riding a bicycle for the first time again and the joyfulness rushed over me. Yes, I was sore and not very nimble. But bicycling was like breathing. It was a natural part of my day. And it was back.

14

Now that the house was on the market in Vero Beach and my body was on the mend, it was time to map out LVSportsBiz.com's charge. The news site was the right product for the right city at the right time with the right person. Las Vegas' sports industry was booming.

In 2016 when I was in Vero Beach, MGM Resorts International and Anschutz Entertainment Group opened T-Mobile Arena behind the New York-New York hotel-casino on the Strip; Nevada Gov. Brian Sandoval signed a legislature-approved bill that earmarked $750 million in public money for a new NFL Raiders' $1.8 billion domed stadium near the Strip; and Las Vegas-based Ultimate Fighting Championship (UFC) -- the MMA fight show and promotions production organization -- was sold by the Fertita brothers for a mind-blowing $4.2 billion.

And that was just for starters. Las Vegas Motor Speedway, the sprawling car racing site on the north end of the Las Vegas metro area, was planning a second annual NASCAR race weekend for September 2018. I didn't know this at the time when I was plotting to return to Las Vegas, but later in 2017 a professional soccer businessman, Brett Lashbrook, received permission from United Soccer League and the city of Las Vegas to launch a professional soccer team called the Las Vegas Lights FC that would play at Cashman Field in downtown Las Vegas.

Meanwhile later in 2017, MGM Resorts International, hungry for an NBA team to be a tenant at T-Mobile Arena along with the NHL team and UFC, bought the WNBA San Antonio Stars and moved the women's basketball club to the Mandalay Bay Events Center on the Strip to start play in 2018.

MGM Resorts rebranded the team into the Las Vegas Aces and invested $10 million into renovating Mandalay Bay Events Center, which received new seats and a new center-hung scoreboard.

Wait, there's more. UNLV hired a new athletic director, Desiree Reed-Francois, and she infused the university's sports programs with enthusiasm and new sports marketing strategies. UNLV dumped IMG College as its sports marketing agency and hired Learfield Communications as its new sports marketing partner under a 10-year deal starting in 2017. UNLV also broke ground on a $31 million football training center on campus thanks to those Fertitta brothers, who controlled the local Station Casinos hotel company and who had just sold UFC for more than $4 billion.

And Las Vegas was emerging as a co-hub with Los Angeles as the epicenter for the exploding esports industry. Companies led by investors ranging from music industry leader and DJ Steve Aoki to former Los Angeles Lakers player Rick Fox were planting the video game competition flag in the ground in Las Vegas. Hundreds of millennials who were the world's best video game players were descending on Las Vegas for all types of competitions in newly-renovated, high-tech, computer screen-filled venues.

Even the Triple A baseball team in Las Vegas was building a new ballyard. The club's owner, Howard Hughes Corporation, which was the master developer for the vast Summerlin master plan community in the metro area's western suburbs, was building a $150 million,10,000-seat minor league ballpark thanks to an $80 million naming rights sponsorship from the area's public tourism agency, the Las Vegas Convention and Visitors Authority. The convention and visitors authority's naming rights deal for Howard Hughes Corp. was ridiculously high ($80 million!) and Howard Hughes executives celebrated with glee after the LVCVA board approved that payout the morning of Oct. 10, 2017.

Las Vegas still had its other big annual sports events, too -- the National Finals Rodeo, when the country's Western and country lifestyle communities came to Las Vegas for nearly two weeks in December for the Super Bowl of rodeos; the PGA golf circuit stop called the Shriners Hospitals for Children Open in Summerlin, where the Tampa, Fla.-based Shriners used the pro golf tourney as a fund-raising catalyst every autumn; and the NBA Summer League, spending 11 days at UNLV's Thomas & Mack Center, where all 30 NBA teams showcased their young players in games during a national and international hoops extravaganza that has evolved into the Woodstock of professional basketball.

LVSportsBiz.com was the right platform to report on this exploding sports industry in Las Vegas.

I still had my network of sports-business contacts in Las Vegas to help me launch the new site. And I had newspaper experience of covering public NFL stadium boards in Denver and Tampa, so I had institutional knowledge and a sense of the political culture surrounding these public panels that typically are made up of local business leaders who function as civic cheerleaders for the NFL team and its stadium plans.

I also had launched a sports-business website for FOX Sports in 2000, so I had a feel for what it's like to start a site that focused on the business side of sports. And here was my secret sauce -- I would apply my old-school, city hall and business newspaper reporter skills to a sector that typically draws feature-oriented coverage. I would make LVSports-Biz.com all about covering everything outside the field, the rink, the court and focus on news and business angles that other news agencies would tend not to look for.

My stories would be news pieces based on information gathered at the intersection of business, politics, sports, stadiums, fan issues, marketing and economic development. I was not be a sports writer. That was not my objective. I was a news and business journalist applying town hall news criteria to story ideas that just happened to be in the sports arena and not in city hall.

As a rule, the goal was to report and write a story for LVSportsBiz.com that would meet one of three news criteria -- it had to be a news scoop, an enterprise piece or an industry insider analysis article. The point was to deliver content in Las Vegas that people could not find anywhere else.

Las Vegas already had several TV stations, a daily newspaper, sports bloggers and an array of social media folks generating stories that would spill into the sports-business category. My aim was to be first, accurate and insightful while delivering journalism in a story-writing tone that was conversational. The press release? I would only report press release news when I absolutely had no other choice. I have an unofficial mantra for LVSportsBiz.com.

The press release equals death. My news site would be all about original content -- breaking news, reporting topics with fresh enterprise angles and writing analytical insider material that would make LVSportsBiz.com a must-read even for people who didn't necessarily even like sports.

15

Newspaper friends are the best. About a month after the crash, Mark Obmascik from the Denver Post visited and planted the seed for LVSportsBiz.com. And then another newspaper friend came by Vero Beach to visit -- and stay two weeks as she moved to Florida for a new job at the Orlando Sentinel. I had worked with Adelaide Chen at the Las Vegas Review-Journal before she got a new job at the Orlando daily paper as a data/multimedia specialist.

She helped me with the design of the website. She helped me pick a WordPress template to serve as the digital home for LVSportsBiz.com. And a Tampa friend, James Villa, created the LVSportsBiz.com logo for the home page. It would be a silhouette of a stadium with LVSportsBiz.com lettering in gold and green.

My mid-May 2017, the return to Las Vegas; the sale of my Vero Beach house; the conception of LVSportsBiz.com; and the slow physical recovery from getting blasted on my bicycle by an admitted distracted and drowsy motorist were crystalizing into a game plan.

By now, I was liquidating everything from my Vero Beach house. Every piece of furniture was sold via Craig's

List. I donated books, clothing, kitchen supplies. The purge felt wonderful. It's embarrassing to collect so much stuff over a lifetime and drag it from place to place. Ridding myself of this material world was liberating. You should try it. Finding emotional security in hoarding so much stuff weighs down on your spirit. Less is more in life.

To move, I mailed seven boxes of personal items to Fisher's bike shop in Las Vegas. And the rest would have to fit in my Kia Soul for the drive back to Las Vegas in late May 2017. The only thing returning to Las Vegas with me would be two bicycles, several boxes that were jammed into my car, files that included the two-page crash report and my 17-year-old pug named Pugsy, who had endured the cross-country car ride from Las Vegas to Vero Beach less than 15 months earlier.

On May 28, 2017, Pugsy would be back in the car's navigator seat in her bed for the 2,500-mile car ride back to the desert and mountains of southern Nevada.

Pugsy on the road

16

I accepted an offer on my house and the closing would take place after I had returned to Las Vegas. And though I was in Vero Beach, I began writing the first group of stories that would inaugurate LVSportsBiz.com's home page. One of the original batch of LVSportsBiz.com stories was a piece on whether Steve Sisolak was a Clark County commissioner or Clark County's sports commissioner because he was such a big Raiders fan and a fan of the new Las Vegas NHL team.

The story focused on whether Sisolak could keep apart his two personas -- the public policy-shaping county commissioner who renders decisions on Raiders stadium issues such as land development plans and parking proposals and the local Raiders fan who posed for a photograph with Raiders cheerleaders on the Strip for an NFL player draft photo opp.

Steve Sisolak.   Photo credit: Daniel Clark

It's an example of the type of story I was striving for --
a unique angle on a sports industry-related subject that had
a topical edge to it that nobody else would be reporting. As
I dove into the launch of LVSportsBiz.com, I realized that
conceiving and executing the news site was the start of my
emotional healing after nearly being killed by a person driving a car who was not held accountable for his actions.

It was providing a mental anchor for me and forcing
me to look ahead and avoid looking in the rear-view mirror
and getting stuck in the trauma. Returning to my roots as a
journalist covering the sports-business industry put Vero
Beach, the failed Florida tours and the crash behind me.

This was a serious news endeavor and it required a new-found focus and purpose. By Sunday May 28, 2017, my house was cleared out. The car was packed. I had a 3 p.m. departure time arranged in my head. It was a simple car ride. Drive north to Interstate 10 in north Florida, turn left and don't stop until I hit Phoenix for the final leg to Las Vegas. I was eager to leave. By 2:40 p.m. Sunday, I was ready 20 minutes before blastoff. I pulled out of the driveway and never looked back.

17

I wanted to leave Florida so badly and get back to Las Vegas that I drove through the night and the early morning so that I could be in another state by the time dawn broke on Monday. I drove across the Florida Panhandle in an interstate vacuum of blackness until I crossed into Alabama and through the South to New Orleans and Houston.

I just kept driving. Once I drove through Houston, I stopped at a Love's truck center and fed Pugsy a bowl filled with her beloved chicken pot pie that smelled better than the grub I was eating along the way. On that Monday night in late May, two hours west of San Antonio, in the Texas hills, I pulled off I-10 and got a room at a Motel 6. Pugsy ate more chicken pot pie.

And I enjoyed the fact that just a mere day after leaving Vero Beach I was already in the middle of Texas. On Tuesday morning, it was back on the interstate for points west -- El Paso; New Mexico; and Tucson, Arizona. On Tuesday night, east of Phoenix, in another Motel 6, I set up camp in the motel room and plotted road strategy for my ride through Phoenix in the early, pre-commute, pre-sunrise hours and then north through the high desert to Las Vegas.

Pugsy and I were ready to roll at 3 a.m. May 31. We beat the Phoenix morning commute on Interstate 10 and then made a right turn and headed north on a road that would take us to Las Vegas. Around 10 a.m. on that Wednesday, I pulled into the Las Vegas Cyclery parking lot. I saw Shawn the store manager and introduced Pugsy to Shawn's ancient little critter, also a dog in the twilight of her life that stayed in Shawn's office.

My re-entry into Las Vegas would be buffered by a two-month house-watching stint thanks to my beer-drinking pal Liz Bash, a geography teacher in the local Clark County school district in Las Vegas who had a friend who needed her central Las Vegas house watched. Liz's friend, Dawn Anderson, would be staying with her parents in Utah, so Pugsy and I set up shop at her house for June and July in 2017.

It was a swirl of emotions returning to Las Vegas after a 14-month sabbatical in Vero Beach. I knew I would be launching LVSportsBiz.com in a week or so and I needed to find advertising income to pay the bills and buy food. I had faith that if I generated terrific content and web traffic, then the ad dollars would follow. I was excited about returning to the news business in Las Vegas, seeing former Review-Journal mates in the field and cranking copy on my own schedule.

18

A week after moving into Dawn Anderson's house to babysit her home, I went live with LVSportsBiz.com in early June 2017.

The initial web traffic was awful. Some people knew I was back in town, but I owe a debt of gratitude to Joe Maloof, the founding partner of the Vegas Golden Knights NHL club and all-around sports dude who believed in LVSportsBiz.com from the start.

I had lunch with Maloof and his sports marketing guy, Kevin Kaplan, to finalize the Maloofs' ad spot on the site. It was a home page strip ad for their Never Too Hungover drink, which Maloof and his brothers later rebranded into "Drinkeade."

I'll never forget Maloof's look on his face when he asked me how many readers did LVSportsBiz.com have at the time during the first month. "Maybe 37 or so," I told him.

I read his face and his body language and his overall look said, "Man, that sucks." But he told me over lunch in actual words, "Don't worry, it's just the start. You'll grow it."

Maloof was right. I did grow it. By October 2018, LVSportsBiz.com's readership had cracked the 130,000 reader barrier and September 2018's web traffic was the site's best ever. But back in June 2017, the Maloofs' ad was the first one and it helped me pay the bills and make the news site financially sustainable into its second year. Thanks for believing in LVSportsBiz.com, Joe. Your faith in me and LVSportsBiz.com was part of my healing process, too.

19

Joe Maloof and brother Gavin contacted homeowner title insurance businessman Bill Foley in December 2013 about creating an NHL team in Las Vegas. A year later in December 2014, NHL Commissioner Gary Bettman gave Foley the green light to pursue a season ticket deposit campaign to see if Las Vegas was up to the challenge of supporting a big-league hockey team.

Of all the many topics I would report on for LVSports-Biz.com, I knew the launch of the Vegas Golden Knights and the construction of the Raiders stadium would be the two hottest flashpoint issues. I met Foley in January 2015 when I working at the Las Vegas Review-Journal and he told me he was confident Las Vegas' market numbers would deliver the initial goal of 10,000 season ticket commitments.

Interviewing Vegas Golden Knights owner Bill Foley.
Photo credit: Daniel Clark

The man who made millions of dollars in the property title insurance business told me there were 130,000 "avid hockey fans" who had annual incomes of at least $55,000 in the Las Vegas market. That base of fans with money to spend on hockey emboldened Foley to sell the idea of a team to the NHL.

On Feb. 10, 2015, I saw Bettman and Bill Foley quietly chatting in an MGM Grand casino-hotel hallway nook. An hour later, Bettman told a packed room at MGM Grand that he officially endorsed Foley's season ticket deposit campaign to gauge the extent to which Las Vegas would back an NHL team in the desert.

On that very same day, after Joe and Gavin Maloof joined Foley at the Bettman announcement event, Las Vegas' hockey fans started making season ticket deposits of $150 to $900 on a website called vegaswantshockey.com.

Back in early 2015, Foley had told me he would be "shocked" if the campaign collected at least 10,000 commitments and NHL didn't award Las Vegas a team. "It would be a big advantage to be the first professional franchise in Las Vegas," Foley let me know at the time.

That type of confidence from Foley, a 1967 West Point graduate, prompted Bettman to tell me in February 2015 that he privately advised Foley to not be so cocky about thinking that 10,000 season ticket deposits would automatically translate into a NHL franchise in Las Vegas.

"What you're hearing is Bill's enthusiasm," Bettman told me in 2015.

Fast forward to June 2017 when I back in Las Vegas. The NHL was unveiling its new adidas jerseys -- including the new Golden Knights sweater -- and I saw Foley and Bettman on this June day at a fancy bar at the Wynn hotel-casino. It was my first major sports-business event since returning to Las Vegas and it was slightly disorienting to be back on the beat. But the point was that I was back. And there was Foley, in jacket and tie. He was on my radar and I stalked him for about 20 feet or so until I caught up with him.

"Hey Bill, how's it going? Remember me?" I asked Foley if I could grab a photo of him in front of the NHL's hockey locker display showing all the new adidas team jerseys, including the new Golden Knights jersey just unveiled. It was just Foley and I at the hockey jersey display.

And it felt good to score an exclusive photo of the Golden Knights owner -- a guy I reported on before my ill-fated Vero Beach sabbatical -- with his team's spanking new hockey jersey. The thrill of journalism was back. I raced back to the house I was sitting and published the only news report that day in Las Vegas showing Foley and the Golden Knights jersey. The scoop felt good.

I was back in the groove. The healing through my website and through reporting was working.

20

Indeed, reporting the Cinderella story of the Vegas Golden Knights helped me heal after the March 7, 2017 crash. Nobody at that NHL event at the Wynn hotel knew that a distracted driver nearly killed me only a few months earlier. But returning to chronicle the business launch of this new NHL team gave my life structure and purpose as LVSportsBiz.com piled up page views and readers in its first year.

I took at look LVSportsBiz.com's back files and there are 20 pages of Vegas Golden Knights stories. At least one-fourth of all the stories published on the site are about the Knights. The team was starting from scratch and I had returned to Las Vegas just in time to attend the team expansion draft at T-Mobile Arena a mere day after I photographed Foley with his new Golden Knights jersey.

I wasn't on the media list to get in to the expansion draft event, so I emailed and messaged NHL head PR man Frank Brown about getting the green light to cover the story. Finally, an NHL PR guy came with a credential, I passed through security and I was in. Foley was on stage reading the names of players from every team in the NHL who were picked by Golden Knights General Manager George McPhee to form the new squad for Las Vegas' first-ever professional major-league team.

The biggest name was goaltender Marc-Andre Fleury, a three-time Stanley Cup winner plucked from the Pittsburgh Penguins.

A player with strong Las Vegas roots was defenseman Deryk Engelland, a former Las Vegas minor league player with the Las Vegas Wranglers who had settled with his family in Las Vegas. He was picked off the Calgary Flames roster.

All cell phones on future Hall-of-Fame goaltender Marc-Andre Fleury at the Vegas Golden Knights expansion draft in June 2017. Photo credit: Alan Snel

The players kept coming. A guy with great flowing hair named William Karlsson from the Columbus Blue Jackets. A fun, chatty dude named Nate Schmidt from the Washington Capitals, where Golden Knights GM McPhee previously worked as a longtime general manager. A short player with a mighty engine named Jonathan Marchessault from the Florida Panthers.

Foley wanted an exciting team that would be competitive in its first year -- or at least entertaining. McPhee's roster of "Misfits," as they were nicknamed, ended up producing a team that was more than just competitive. The mashup of all these players created a team that would make history. And I was there to document the business side of all this. The serendipity of the birth of the Golden Knights' roster and the LVSportsBiz.com website was wonderful.

21

The Maloofs were back to their old fun ways in Las Vegas. The Maloof boys were all never-married bachelors and sports were just part of their fun.

In August 2017, I received a call from Kevin Kaplan, the Maloofs' sports marketing man who helped me settle on the LVSportsBiz.com name when I was living back in Vero Beach. He told me on this August day that he would have a mind-blowing story for me for LVSportsBiz.com in a few hours.

Hang tight, he advised. I called Kaplan several hours later and LVSportsBiz.com received a monster news scoop that put us on the sports-business website map. On this day, Aug. 12, 2017, Kaplan told me that it was Joe and Gavin Maloof who were the anonymous bettors who had waged a stunning $880,000 on local Las Vegas boxing champ Floyd Mayweather to beat UFC star Conor McGregor in the much-hyped crossover boxing spectacle at T-Mobile Arena that matched the undefeated boxer against the well-known MMA personality in a "sportstainment" event that made tens of millions of dollars for both.

During the week leading up to my LVSportsBiz.com scoop, there were headline-grabbing news reports about the anonymous sports gambler who placed the $880,000 bet on Mayweather to win. At the time, the $880,000 bet at South Point hotel was believed to be the biggest wager on the fight. Mayweather was a -550 favorite to beat McGregor. If Mayweather won, it would net the Maloof brothers $160,000 -- money the family wanted to donate to charity.

The sports gambling beat is a giant news category, especially in Las Vegas where sports gambling is its own entertainment category and generates tens of millions of dollars for the state of Nevada. Thanks to the big scoop, LVSPortsBiz.com traffic and views soared and the news site became a news source player on the Las Vegas scene. After low view numbers in June and July of 2017, monthly views for August skyrocketed more than 550 percent.

I appreciated a former Review-Journal colleague, RJ sports gambling reporter Todd Dewey, who credited LVSportsBiz.com with breaking the news in his story on the Maloofs' placing the bet. But the Associated Press, which has a policy of crediting news organizations for breaking news when AP follows the story, stiffed LVSportsBiz.com and did not include a line citing LVSportsBiz for first reporting the news. I contacted the AP writer, Greg Beacham, and his editors at the news service to please include a line citing LVSportsBiz.com for first reporting the news. But the AP gave no response -- just crickets. But it didn't matter. It was August, my third month on the LVSportsBiz.com beat, and the news site began getting traction.

22

It was six months after the crash trauma and it had altered the places where I rode my bicycle. I used to bike everywhere on my bicycle -- and that's no hyperbole. I rode my bicycle across the country twice solo and used my bicycle to commute from northern New Jersey to my old FOXSports-Biz.com job in Manhattan, where I survived biking thousands of miles through a web of New York drivers and taxi operators back in 2000.

I rode my bicycle in high-crash metro areas in South Florida and Tampa Bay, and bicycled in every corner of the country from Seattle to Southern California to metro New York to Florida and figured if someone operating a motorized vehicle could drive on a road then I had the same right to drive my human-powered vehicle.

But a motorist on a quiet, two-lane road outside Fort Pierce changed my mindset. No matter how safe I rode my bicycle, I was still vulnerable to incompetent, distracted or speeding motorists. I have a daily ritual of making sure my bed was made before I went out for my daily bicycle ride. The reason is that if I was killed while bicycling, I didn't want my sister Debbie to come to my home and see an un-made bed.

Sadly, I accepted the pathetic reality that our country casually accepts the thousands of bicyclist and pedestrian deaths at the hands of so many motorists who drive too fast, are too impatient and made decisions on the road that result in crashes into bicyclists and walkers. Literally thousands of bicyclists are struck by motorists in this country every year and they're viewed by everyone from road engineers to elected officials to public works supervisors to police as the unavoidable collateral damage of car operators doing their daily business on America's roads.

I have reached a simple conclusion -- the way we teach, license and regulate people who operate motorized vehicles is broken. And that not much will change until we overhaul the manner in which our country educates people to operate cars and punishes people for using vehicles that are involved in maiming and killing innocent pedestrians and bicyclists.

The driver who nearly killed me changed my approach to bicycling. I can longer trust people who drive cars to navigate around me when we're co-users on the roads. No other people in this country are more trusting than bicyclists. We place our trust in people we don't know to properly navigate their motorized vehicles around us when we are on the roadways together. Sadly and regrettably, I learned the hard way that motorists don't always do that.

These days, I mostly ride my bicycle on a route that has a road shoulder that takes me to the inspiring Red Rock Canyon road loop run by the federal Bureau of Land Management.

I don't ride my bicycle on the roads around Las Vegas as much as I used to. I still take an occasional bike ride down the famed and bicycle-unfriendly Strip, but I take the ride on Sunday mornings around 8 a.m. when traffic is light. When I do ride the Strip, I always remember the legacy of bicyclist Matthew Hunt, who was killed while leading a bicycle tour on the Strip three years ago. I have become friends with Hunt's mother, Cynthia Finnegan of upstate New York, because she continues to keep her son's memory alive through her many daily bike rides and an annual ride in his memory here in Las Vegas.

People who operate motorized vehicles are encapsulated by metal and bumpers. People who operate bicycles have the protection of a bicycle helmet and not much more.

Bicycling the Red Rock scenic drive.   Photo credit: Alan Snel

A stop along the Red Rock scenic drive.   Photo credit: Alan Snel

A crash between motorist and bicyclist -- even one that is not necessarily violent -- can end a bicyclist's life. Motorists and bicyclists both use our public roads, yet there is often disagreement on where people believe bicyclists should be positioned in the road. Here's my best advice: if you drive a car, look at a bicyclist as simply a slow-moving vehicle and take proper steps to safely drive your vehicle around the bicyclist. There is a false equivalent of concerns by the motorist and bicyclist.

The motorist gets angry because he believes the bicyclist is slowing him down. The bicyclist gets angry because his life is at stake when a motorist makes a mistake. Yet, we're in this together. Government will not build a separate bicycle trail outside of every public roadway.

So far now, people who operate motorized vehicles and people who ride bicycles are co-users of the same public right-of-ways and I can only make this plea to motorists: Focus on operating your vehicles in a way that will not kill a vulnerable bicyclist or pedestrian.

23

The Vegas Golden Knights were the Las Vegas market's first major-league team. So, they were a cornerstone of LVSportsBiz.com's content.

I knew owner Foley from my days of working at the Review-Journal. But I did not know the team's president, Kerry Bubolz, nor the team's first chief marketing officer, Nehme Abouzeid.

My first major story on the Golden Knights was a piece on Bubolz and how he would launch hockey in the non-traditional desert market of southern Nevada, with a story focus on youth hockey programs to plant the seeds of the next generation of Knights fans in Las Vegas.

I contacted Bubolz's assistant to arrange an appointment. She emailed me back to advise that I could talk with Bubolz at 5 p.m. on a day in early July. But there was a mixup. When I showed up, Bubolz's assistant said I was not scheduled to see him.

Vegas Golden Knights President Kerry Bubolz.
Photo credit: Daniel Clark

Just about every major-league team I covered in markets around the country would have told me to come back another day. But the Golden Knights were different.

Bubolz told me to hang around. He would see me after he was done with a meeting. I waited about a half-hour. And true to his word, Bubolz came down the steps from his second-floor office and told me to come up with him. We talked for about 30 minutes about the Golden Knights' marketing plan to grow hockey in the sunbelt. The Knights already had 14,0000 season ticket equivalents to help fill T-Mobile Arena's 18,000 seats, so it was not like Bubolz would be stressed out to fill the venue.

But he did need to form the marketing foundation for a new franchise, which would also need to create revenue streams in sponsorships, media rights and merchandise sales.

Here's how life works. More than a year later in August 2018, I had to call up that story to recall the details of that Bubolz interview. But I had no problem recalling how I felt when the team president in the midst of building a big-league team from scratch found time to talk to me when I didn't have an appointment because of the scheduling confusion. It was an early clue this first-year team would be a little different than other major-league clubs.

24

I first fell in love with this sports-business beat when I covered the intersection of city hall and stadiums in Denver, when the Broncos received money from a Colorado legislature-approved sales tax collected by a regional six-county tax district in metro Denver.

I was fascinated that billionaires who owned big-league teams could saunter into the halls of government and walk away with public subsidies to build stadiums that produced revenues for them. So, I was eager in June 2017 to attend my first public stadium board meeting in Las Vegas, where the Raiders were receiving a $750 million subsidy to help build their domed, 65,000-seat stadium on 62 acres on the west side of Interstate 15, across the highway from Mandalay Bay hotel-casino on the southern end of the Strip.

The stadium board was chaired by a former concrete company owner named Steve Hill, who was the economic development chief for Governor Brian Sandoval at the time and would later become the COO/president of the Las Vegas Convention and Visitors Authority, Las Vegas' public tourism agency.

UNLV had looked at building a similar domed stadium on its campus two miles to the east of the Raiders stadium site-- but that was before the Raiders had decided to leave Oakland. Now with the NFL owners approving the Raiders' move to Las Vegas, the NFL team was playing out the string in Oakland and would set up shop in the new stadium in 2020. The Raiders were also building a $100 million training center in neighboring Henderson, the Second City in the Las Vegas metro market.

The local public stadium board consisted of mostly local business types, like MGM Resorts International President Bill Hornbuckle, construction company owner and real estate developer Tito Tiberti and UFC executive Lawrence Epstein.

Laborers Local 872 even had a voice on the stadium board in Raiders superfan Tommy White, who was not shy about exhorting his board mates to get going and start approving all the paperwork necessary to build the $1.8 billion stadium. The southern Nevada public was contributing its $750 million thanks to a hotel bed tax increase in Clark County. More than $1 billion would be raised over 30 years on the debt service for the $750 million.

Covering the stadium meant returning to my happy place, a journalistic safe zone where I can chat with the stadium board's main consultant, a friendly, fact-filled, can-do lawyer by the name of Jeremy Aguero. The 44-year-old fourth-generation Las Vegan literally wrote the state law that is guiding the process behind the Raiders building the venue with stadium authority oversight. Aguero is principal analyst with Applied Analysis, the 21-year-old firm that he founded and that was being paid up to $25,000 a month by the stadium authority for work as needed.

One of my first stadium stories was a focus piece on Aguero.

Aguero did his homework. He digested all the information churned out by Gov. Sandoval's Southern Nevada Tourism Infrastructure Committee during its 16 months of action and then he read lots of NFL stadium agreements for venues for teams such as the Atlanta Falcons, San Francisco 49ers, Minnesota Vikings, Houston Texans and Dallas Cowboys.

And yes, he listened to the Oakland Raiders and their execs like owner Mark Davis and team president Marc Badain.

"They had opinions on several provisions," Aguero told me with a flair for the understatement with that quip.

Writing stadium stories allowed me to ease my transition back to Las Vegas. I was physically healing, but the emotional healing side was catching up.

Raiders stadium consultant and Las Vegas lawyer Jeremy Aguero.
Photo credit: Daniel Clark

Raiders President Marc Badain.   Photo credit: Daniel Clark

I threw myself into reporting and writing on the Golden Knights, the Mayweather-McGregor mega boxing event, the Raiders stadium and the new professional sports teams that would be added to the local market.

And what probably appeared to be dedication to journalism in this dynamic sports-business world in Las Vegas was the cathartic process that allowed me to put the crash and Vero Beach in the rear-view mirror and look forward.

But in retrospect, I looked back from the vantage point of early October 2018 and wonder if I was avoiding coming to terms with my mortality and nearly being killed by burying myself in the endless sports-business stories I wrote. In the first 16 months after I launched LVSportsBiz,com, I had published more than 525 stories.

That's a stunning level of news production. Keep in mind that that's not blog posts or quick-hit opinion hits that can be rattled off in 10 minutes. I took pride in the journalism I published on LVSportsBiz.com and I was often rolling four different jobs into one when I published a story on the site. I was reporter, photographer, website publisher and copy editor all combined into one person.

I began writing this book only when I felt there was enough emotional distance to reflect back on this journey of overcoming trauma, starting to heal, finding a purpose and focusing on moving forward. I can understand why it's so easy to get bogged down after a physical trauma. The physical pain and inability to be mobile can be depressing. Relying on other people and giving up your autonomy can be devastating. Losing your ability to make a living can be a financial hardship.

I had only one strategy to transcend this emotional muck -- throw myself into launching the new site and return to reporting about a news niche that has high-profile relevance in Las Vegas. It gave me the new focus and purpose I needed to move forward and look ahead.

25

My Las Vegas return also allowed me to catch up with a building that I covered during its construction phase. But I had never stepped foot inside it because T-Mobile Arena made its debut while I was in Vero Beach in 2016. I didn't get a look inside T-Mobile Arena until July 17, 2017 when I reported a story on the arena's executive chef, Garry DeLucia, of stadium/arena concessionaire Levy Restaurants.

While I walked and talked with DeLucia along the arena's main concourse and took in the views of the venue's lobby and sponsor signage along the walls, I realized that it was another step in my emotional recovery.

On May 1, 2014, I reported on the arena's groundbreaking and I remember the day well. I wrote the story on site in a tent thanks to wifi courtesy of Michael Roth, the PR chief at Anschutz Entertainment Group (AEG), the Los Angeles-based sports and entertainment company owned by Colorado billionaire Philip Anschutz.

T-Mobile Arena, home of the Vegas Golden Knights and UFC.
Photo credit: Alan Snel

Former MGM Resorts International executive Rick Arpin told me he would install this plaque for all my polite badgering for bike racks at the arena. I thought Arpin was kidding. But he wasn't.

AEG built the arena in partnership with MGM Resorts International, sharing the cost of the $375 million venue. AEG and MGM Resorts each brought $75 million in equity to the table for a down payment of $150 million, so their mortgage was $225 million thanks to a loan by Bank of America.

The Strip was evolving as a sports entertainment mecca with the construction of the arena -- the first major sports venue being built in Las Vegas in 30 years. It also meant big business for MGM Resorts. "It's a big day for Las Vegas. It's a big day for Nevada. It's a big day for entertainment," Murren told the groundbreaking crowd that May 2014 morning. "We need to create the experience tourists are so yearning for. They want to be wowed."

The arena's first tenants would be UFC and the NHL team -- and Murren had his own yearning. He wants an NBA team in the building to generate more dates and revenues. Former basketball star Bill Walton was on hand to serve up some amusing groundbreaking comments in a way that only Walton can. And he relished the fact that his beloved Conference of Champions -- the Pac 12 -- would be holding its basketball tournament in the building every year.

Even Floyd "Money" Mayweather, who enjoyed attending local sporting events with a backpack filled with wads of cash, was part of the groundbreaking ceremony.

Little did Mayweather know at the time he would be fighting the MMA showman McGregor in a spectacle boxing match that was an example of the one-off "sportstainment" events that Las Vegas was ideal at pulling off.

Undefeated boxer Floyd Mayweather at a Las Vegas Aces game.
Photo credit: J. Tyge O'Donnell

By May 27, 2015, the contractor team of Hunt-Penta installed the final beam and the arena project was two days ahead of schedule. The place opened April 6, 2016 with a concert by the Las Vegas-rooted The Killers, Shamir and Wayne Newton. I was in Vero Beach at the time and read the story on the debut online. It hurt to not be there -- to report on the opening of a pivotal building I had reported on for months in Las Vegas.

But here I was on this July day in 2017, strolling the T-Mobile Arena concourse for the first time. Even the most jaded reporter had to be impressed with the interior of the arena, with its wide concourse, tall ceiling and lack of visual commercial clutter on the walls. The upper bowl seats offered terrific sight lines because there was only one level of suites. There were special upscale lounges and seating areas built into the bowl to offer a variety of seat options.

DeLucia, the arena's executive chef, showed me the dishes that would be served for the Golden Knights fans, from the $29.95 buffet to the $13 prime rib sandwich. Before we took the arena culinary tour, DeLucia opened a cabinet file drawer in his Levy Restaurants office and reached for two carving knives to give to a worker. "After you lose 20 of these you better start keeping an eye on them," DeLucia told me. I laughed and we covered a lot of ground in the arena that afternoon.

Only after I began reporting and writing on the Golden Knights, the Raiders stadium and the arena during the summer of 2017 did I understand what it was like to start feeling healed. It was only four months after nearly losing my life in the crash. I was back. I was home as I strolled along the T-Mobile Arena main concourse.

26

When Brophy drove his car into me that March 2017 morning, little did I know that the crash would serve as the catalyst behind my rebirth and a second lease on life in Las Vegas three months later.

There was an emotional rush at returning to report the stories that I had started to document before moving to Florida. It was as if I was being made whole again. The more I poured myself into reporting for LVSportsBiz.com, the more I was putting the crash behind me. So I plugged away at cranking out stories with a different angle on Las Vegas' exploding sports development scene.

But I just didn't focus on catching up on old sports-business developments. There were new people launching new teams in Las Vegas. And that newness of personalities helped my re-birth here in Las Vegas. There was the over-the-top enthusiastic Brett Lashbrook, who was bringing a new professional soccer team to downtown Las Vegas. Lashbrook was from Kansas City where he was named after George Brett. Starting pro soccer in Las Vegas was not his first rodeo. Lashbrook had helped move an Orlando soccer team from the second-tier, Triple A United Soccer League to the big leagues of soccer in this country, Major League Soccer.

Now he was in Las Vegas. And in the summer of 2017 he received approval from the city of Las Vegas to launch a new United Soccer League team in downtown Cashman Field. Las Vegas Mayor Carolyn Goodman made an unsuccessful bid two years earlier for Major League Soccer when she teamed the city with the sports-loving Findlays -- a local car dealership family -- and a development company from Baltimore called The Cordish Companies in hopes of building a publicly-subsidized soccer stadium in downtown. Her husband, Oscar, Las Vegas' former mayor from 1999-2011, tried for years to lure major league sports to Las Vegas.

Carolyn Goodman, who succeeded her colorful, martini-toting husband as mayor in 2011, adopted the jovial Lashbrook as her soccer savior in 2017.Lashbrook, caring for his mom in Las Vegas, had become the Pied Piper for professional soccer in Las Vegas. Carolyn Goodman adored Lashbrook's unbridled enthusiasm and his soccer team plan turned out to be a giant draw for the area's Latino population, which would serve as the biggest demographic group of fans for the new team. His team, though not very successful on the soccer field, was drawing about 7,000 fans a game to downtown Cashman Field in 2018.

Lashbrook was unconventional and refreshingly candid and open about the creation of the new team, allowing fans to name the club. Locals voted online and named the team the Las Vegas Lights FC. Lashbrook found a natural downtown corporate partner in Zappos, the giant online shoe and clothing retailer, which shared a kinship with Lashbrook for the unorthodox. The Zappos name adorned the Lights' colorful uniforms highlighted by streaks of fluorescent pink and blue and Zappos loaned out the call center's llamas for Lights soccer games.

Lashbrook swam against the sports marketing orthodoxy, signing up a marijuana dispensary as a sponsor, starting in-stadium gambling thanks to a partnership with sports gambling giant William Hill and hiring zany coach Jose Luis Sanchez Sola who went by the nickname, El Chelis. Sola ended up quitting with only six games left on the inaugural season schedule and his son ended up coaching the Lights.

My favorite El Chelis stunt was when he was thrown out of a Lights game for mixing it up with an opponent's coach. Sola then lit up a cigarette when he took a seat in the supporters section to watch the finish of the game at Cashman Field.

Another Lights promotion involved a helicopter hovering above Cashman Field at a September 2018 game and dropping $5,000 for 200 fans to gobble up.

Lashbrook intends to update Cashman Field after the minor league baseball team he shares the venue with -- the Howard Hughes Corp.-owned 51s -- moves to Las Vegas' western suburbs to a new $150 million Triple A ballpark in Summerlin in 2019.

Thanks to a strong Latino turnout at Lights games, the Lights ranked among the leaders in attendance in the United Soccer League. Lashbrook's master plan is to move the Lights to Major League Soccer -- a transition he knows from his work in Orlando.

Las Vegas Mayor and Lashbrook supporter Carolyn Goodman.
Photo credit: Erik John Ricardo

Helicopter dropping $5,000 on Las Vegas Lights soccer field for
halftime promotion in 2018.   Photo credit: J. Tyge O'Donnell

27

In the middle of the summer of 2017, Nehme Abouzeid left the Golden Knights as their chief marketing officer and he was replaced by Brian Killingsworth, who held the CMO position at the Tampa Bay Buccaneers. Killingsworth was reunited with his old pal, Jim Frevola, the Golden Knights corporate sponsorships chief who worked with the marketing executive when the duo worked together at the Tampa Bay Bucs.

I thought it was fascinating in a flashy city of big names and hotel-casino owners like Sheldon Adelson, Steve Wynn, the Fertitta family and Michael Gaughan it was a group of outsiders like Bill Foley and a business staff of executives who came from other markets to launch Las Vegas' first major-league team.

LVSportsBiz.com published a long story on how the outsiders built the big-league team. It was a long story and all the reporting about the Golden Knights was helping me get over the crash trauma and move forward. But moving forward from physical trauma means also making strides emotionally, too. The crash made me think hard and long about mortality. And to this day, I wonder why I wasn't killed given the violent nature of the impact by Brophy's car into me and my bicycle.

When I was in Vero Beach after the crash and was at the point of contemplating moving back to Las Vegas, I had several long phone discussions with a terrific Las Vegas friend, Jean Fajardo, a licensed clinical social worker with terrific listening skills who helped me make the emotional transition from Vero Beach to Las Vegas.

My second lease on life was hitched to diving into launching LVSportsBiz.com. I was strategically catching the wave of this historic era in Las Vegas where stadiums were being built and new professional teams were being birthed. The serendipity of the Golden Knights' inaugural season gave me an emotional anchor.

Lee Orchard plays the "knight" at Vegas Golden Knights games.
Photo credit: Daniel Clark

There was an endless line of stories to report from the business side of the Golden Knights' first season. There was also a bubbling excitement to know that I was there in Las Vegas five years earlier to report on Foley's early efforts to bring an NHL team to Las Vegas.

Las Vegas always had major league sports -- a litany of high-profile boxing matches at Caesars; NASCAR's biggest names descending on Las Vegas Motor Speedway's 1.5-mile track; UFC's mixed martial art fighters led by ringmaster Dana White, who turned a trainer's career into a multi-million-dollar job of matchmaking UFC fights and then promoting them; National Finals Rodeo cowboys who packed UNLV's Thomas & Mack Center every December; and professional golf's premier golfers hitting a PGA event on the major-league circuit in Las Vegas every fall.

They were all athletes -- but only one team had united Las Vegas in ways an individual person could not.

UNLV's basketball team under the late Jerry Tarkanian won a national championship in 1990 before the one-and-done basketball era, finishing that season with a wipeout national title game triumph over Duke to finish 35-5. For 27 years after UNLV's national championship, Las Vegas has never had a major-league team to rally around. Well, until 2017 and the Golden Knights.

28

Now that I'm firmly resettled back in Las Vegas, I bike the 13-mile Red Rock National Conservation Area scenic loop several times a week. The stunning natural beauty along the federal-controlled strip of pavement was my outdoor temple. No matter how many times I pedaled the loop's first five steep miles, it was always a reassuring setting for me to meditate and eventually organize the activities of my day.

After the crash, I was grateful to be gazing at these Spring Mountains foothills, where raw, naked rock covered by spiky, high desert vegetation and even splashes of greenery and trees never made me bored.

I loved the shape and contours of this Red Rock land, and gave thanks every time I slowly grinded up the steep grade to the overlook between miles four and five.

It's funny how people think Las Vegas is the Strip and boring desert. I've bicycled in every corner of this country and across the country twice and I'd match Red Rock Canyon, Mount Charleston and Valley of Fire in metro Las Vegas against any trio of natural settings in a metro market in this country.

A stop while bicycling Mount Charleston.   Photo credit: Alan Snel

*Biking the Surly Pugsley fat-tire bike on the Bristlecone Trail on
Mount Charleston.   Photo credit: Alan Snel*

The raw landscapes are nature's sculptures outside Las Vegas. And every time I tell myself to go and visit the Grand Canyon, or the Oregon Coast or Zion National Park, I find myself happy just to bike Mount Charleston and gaze at its alpine veneer, sheer white rocks and unpredictable contour while I pedal under a spell.

My new criteria for happiness was being alive. And all this -- the land, my relationships and the launch of LVSportsBiz.com -- was all gravy. The crash instantly crystallized where I needed to be. Away from Florida and back in southern Nevada where the nature made me feel like I was home.

Sad to say, the act of a careless, inattentive motorist eclipsed many of the positive memories I had of Florida, and reinforced the notion that Florida is a state where bicyclists are second-class citizens. Remember, I tried to share my favorite bicycle rides in the state's most scenic natural settings when I launched the Escape Adventures Florida bike tour business. But, there were not many takers.

I still have many people I care deeply about in Florida and friends from the newspapers I worked at in South Florida, Tampa Bay and Melbourne. But Southern Nevada is my home. During most mornings, I would snap a photo showing a particular scene, angle of rock or shade of light and post it on social media with the #NBW hashtag -- Nature Before Writing.

While many times I bike by myself, sometimes I do bike with my pal, Scott Sofferman, a retired veterinarian and college sciences teacher who has a stable of bicycles at his house a mile from where I live. I don't ride bikes in big groups too much. The bicycle means freedom to pedal wherever you want to go, and stop whenever you want. But big bicycle groups take away that freedom and I often fall prey to my inquisitive style while bicycling where I often will stop on a dime to take a photo or even talk with someone I meet on the side of the road.

After I returned to Las Vegas, I found myself trying to re-establish friendships that were in place when I left Las Vegas in February 2016 and pedaling Dr. Sofferman was at the top of the list.

We ride road bicycles together, wearing those bike shorts and jerseys you see on road cyclists. But the truth is neither one of us are racer types and we bike the Red Rock scenic drive together because we can gab away pedaling side-by-side and motorists can easily pass us in a second lane along the one-way scenic drive.

We would jabber away about everything -- old New York Mets players like Ron Hunt who stood close to the plate so he can reach first base via the hit batsman; eating gluton-free pizza at his Settebello restaurant where the pizza oven came from Italy; and places where he enjoyed bicycling like Utah and Alaska.

I live in Summerlin, a large sprawling master planned community built by Howard Hughes Corporation on the west side of Las Vegas Valley. Its geographic location is why I live here. It's at the gateway to Red Rock Canyon and I bike a mere six miles to the scenic loop entrance, about 20 miles or so west of the Strip.

Howard Hughes Corp. promoted Summerlin with pretty photos of bicyclist scenes and sold neighborhoods based on the healthy lifestyle theme. But as much as bicycling was a physical activity, the daily bike ride through Red Rock Canyon was the emotional and mental anchor to my day.

It was bike by morning and Golden Knights by afternoon and night for LVSportsBiz.com. The Golden Knights -- because they were a new team with plenty of sports-business news angles -- kept me going and served as the anchor for LVSportsBiz.com during the summer of 2017.

There was my early interview of Jonny Greco, an easy-going team VP who was the head of the team's in-game entertainment -- the game ops. The Golden Knights received lots of news attention for their pregame shows and Vegas acts between periods, And Greco was the coach behind the entertainment outside of the game itself.

Like so many of the Golden Knights' off-ice staff, he was an import with a long resume that included working at the WWE, the Cleveland Cavaliers, the NFL Pro Bowl, the NHL Columbus Blue Jackets, MLB's Miami Marlins and even the Olympics and Carnival Cruises.

Something told me Greco would have fun showcasing Las Vegas' entertainment themes at Vegas Golden Knights games. He used his mental file cabinet of movie scenes and musical scores to create the over-the-top, theatrical, in-game entertainment with a crew that fashioned the ideas with yellow post-it notes

Story by story, I was forming the foundation of my business reporting relationship with the Golden Knights and I was ready to go when pre-season games began in September.

On the final day of September, a person died who ended up changing my life but whom I never ending up meeting.

Dennis Brophy, the driver who operated the Chevy Cruze that slammed into me, died Sept, 30, 2017. I never did hear a word from Brophy after he drove his car into me. From his obituary, I learned some things about him that made him more human to me besides being the name of a person on a police crash report. He was born in Brooklyn, NY -- where I was born. Brophy was born on Oct. 22, 1952 -

- about nine years before I was born. He and his mom moved to Vero Beach in 1986 after his father died. His mother died in 2000. In 2005, Brophy graduated from Nova South University with a Master's degree. He then got a job at New Horizons of the Treasure Coast as a Licensed Mental Health Counselor. Before he died, Brophy had joined Good News Missionary Baptist Church in Fort Pierce. Even though he drove a car into me that nearly took my life, I wanted to let you know who this guy was even if he never reached out to me to apologize. The day after Brophy died, I covered the Golden Knights' final pre-season match against the San Jose Sharks.

The score, for the record, was 5-3 in favor of the Sharks. The game ended about 8 p.m. The game's date was Oct. 1, 2017.

29

Las Vegas would never be the same. At 10:05 p.m. Oct. 1, a madman armed with rapid-fire weaponry and ammo set up shop in a 32nd floor corner suite at Mandalay Bay hotel-casino and fired round after round after round, taking out innocent country music festival fans across the street along the Strip a mere-quarter mile away at MGM Resorts' festival grounds.

It was an 11-minute shooting spree and the deadliest mass shooting by an individual in U.S. history, resulting in 58 people losing their lives at the Route 91 Harvest country music event and more than 500 other people injured from the shooting slaughter.

The Golden Knights pre-season game had ended only two hours earlier. I wrote a Golden Knights-Sharks business story for LVSportsBiz.com earlier in the evening and drove through the Las Vegas Boulevard-Tropicana Avenue an hour before the mass shooting began.

I was home when I turned on the news and saw chaos on the Strip. Mass shootings happen all across America. Now the Las Vegas Strip was among them. The soundtrack was rapid-fire gunfire. It's what America is known for around the world -- the country where people buy weapons of war and store enough ammo to stock a small army to kill innocent people at schools, movie houses and now music festivals on one of the country's most well-known roads.

The mass shooting killings have become so common in America that there's a script to follow -- the thoughts and prayers from Washington, D.C.; the public debate on why there's easy access to weaponry that can kill so many people so fast; and the hashtag slogans of #YourHometownStrong that appears suddenly everywhere from car bumpers to sides of buildings; the massive impromptu memorials showing photos of smiling faces of innocent people gunned down with mounds of flowers decorating the haunting roadside displays.

The Vegas Golden Knights' season opened five days later in Dallas and the home-opener was Oct. 10. Less than 48 hours after the mass killing, Golden Knights players were making the rounds to first responders at Las Vegas Metropolitan Police Department, victims' family members at the Las Vegas Convention Center and blood donors at the United Blood Services center in central Las Vegas.

Former Golden Knights goaltender Calvin Pickard was at the blood donation center. The former Golden Knights player who was traded to the Toronto Maple Leafs before the inaugural season started put it best that day only 48 hours after the slaughter on the Strip: "There's more to life than hockey right now."

The Golden Knights' most high-profile player is goalie Marc-Andre Fleury, known for his omnipresent smile and joking ways.

But Fleury, like his teammates, stood in a semi-circle around country music concert attendee Courtney Oldenburg as she tearfully explained to the players what she endured when she heard the rapid-fire pop-pop-pop of assault rifle bullets flying by her and tried to figure out where the gunfire was coming from.

"The thing I remember most was my boyfriend pushing me to the ground and telling him I love him and wondering if those were the last words I would ever say," Oldenburg told a steely-faced Fleury.

The goalie, a prankster known for his funny quips in the locker room, stood silent and then wrapped his arms around the young woman.

There was nothing more that could be done at that moment. "The fact they take time out of their busy schedules lifts my heart," Oldenburg said. "I'm sure these people had more important things to do today."

Vegas Golden Knights goaltender Marc-Andre Fleury listening to an Oct. 1 festival survivor in the days after the mass shooting on the Strip. Photo credit: Alan Snel

Actually, they didn't. "It's surreal. You never think about being part of this," former Golden Knights player Brendan Leipsic said at the blood donation center. "I was at the Cosmopolitan. We were locked down. You never think you'll be in that situation."

But they were. And now Las Vegas was regrettably grouped among America's other mass shootings with the heartbreaking distinction of being the deadliest of all.

Blood donor Dean Roberts was at the blood center and and said the Golden Knights' appearance meant a lot to him. "This is showing that this is their home. They are not bullshitting. They care and you can tell by talking with them," Roberts said.

Massachusetts State Trooper Phil Giardino waited to give blood and recalled local Boston sports team players helping lift the spirits of Bostonians after the 2013 Boston Marathon bombing. He was in Las Vegas for a conference and decided to donate blood to help the shooting massacre victims.

"Any time there's a sports franchise getting involved, it's great for the city and the sport," Giardino said. "No one forced them to come out."

The Golden Knights players were selected by the first-year NHL franchise less than five months earlier, yet here they were, chatting with people they had never met as blood was donated for the injured. "It's time to come together as a city," Golden Knights defenseman Brayden McNabb said. "Just being here, I hope it helps."

Three days later, the Golden Knights players were playing the team's first-ever game in Dallas.

30

Las Vegas coped the best that people could. It's a metro area of 2.3 million people. But there's a handful of people who call the shots and everyone knows somebody who knows that person that you may know. The Golden Knights did their part, winning their first ever game, 2-1, thanks to veteran James Neal's winner with less than three minutes to play.

Then it was off to Arizona and the Knights won again, 2-1. This time, the Knights knotted the score with a little more than a minute left in regulation. And then it was that Neal guy again, scoring the game-winning goal in overtime for a second consecutive 2-1 victory.

All the while, the front office staff was planning the Oct. 10 home-opener, which would take place a mere nine days after the nation's deadliest mass shooting. The first home game at T-Mobile Arena would be a delicate balancing act between marking the franchise's historic first home game and honoring the memories of the 58 people killed Oct. 1. A fanfest had already been postponed because a hockey festival to stoke the fires of Golden Knights fans was emotionally out of place in a city that needed emotional healing.

There were subdued emotions with a touch of excitement as the Golden Knights coaches and the team's executives followed a red carpet into the arena. Along with team president Kerry Bubolz, corporate sales chief Frevola and CMO Killingsworth, there were Blue Man Group, NHL Commissioner Gary Bettman and hundreds of fans crammed along the red carpet getting pucks and jerseys signed.

"It's overwhelming. The fan support has been unbelievable," Killingsworth told me that day. "All of us are extremely excited and it's going to be really emotional for the Vegas Golden Knights and the city of Las Vegas."

Once inside, the anticipation and excitement blended with healing and sorrow over the shooting and the Golden Knights struck the right chord with a pre-game ceremony that I recall with goose bumps. Cops, firefighters, nurses, medics, doctors and dispatchers were individually matched with Golden Knights players in a powerful pre-game ceremony.

Emotional home season opener for Vegas Golden Knights at
T-Mobile Arena Oct. 10.   Photo credit: Daniel Clark

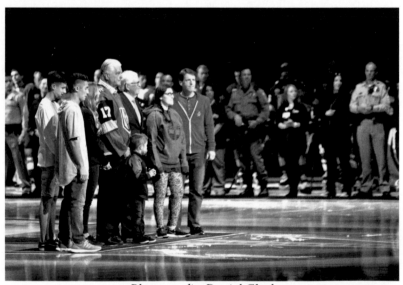

Photo credit: Daniel Clark

Photo credit: Daniel Clark

Greco, the team's entertainment chief, hit the right notes with a program that was part-healing, part-inspirational, part-tribal gathering after metro Las Vegas suffered so many losses and emotional traumas from a gunman's savage attack on the Strip nine days earlier.

"It was a night everyone in this arena will remember for the rest of their lives," said Joe Maloof, the founding partner who attended the first game with his brother, Gavin. "It was beautiful. You have just so many moments to cherish in your life and this is one of them."

The team's elder statesman, defenseman Deryk Engelland had a home in metro Las Vegas after playing for the minor league Wranglers in town. Engelland gave a heartwarming speech to a crowd that needed a reason to cheer after a sorrowful nine days.

His Vegas Strong speech was simple and eloquent and much shorter than what team staff had originally written for him. Engelland said the original script was too long to memorize and he noted his wife helped craft the speech that gave an emotional jolt in much the same way former Boston Red Sox star David "Big Papi" ignited the emotions of Boston folks at Fenway Park in the aftermath of the Boston Marathon bombing in April 2013.

There were 58 seconds of silence - a second for each victim killed -- before the puck was dropped. "It was a powerful moment when we bowed our heads for the 58 seconds," Joe Maloof told me that night. "It was serene, peaceful and powerful all at the same time."

Clark County Commission Chairman Steve Sisolak, the Democratic nominee for Nevada governor in 2018, was part of the emotionally-charged pre-game ceremony where he stood on the ice with first responders and survivors.

"You're mixing a terrible tragedy with something we've been waiting for two years to happen," Sisolak said to me as we strolled the main concourse. Sisolak, a big Golden Knights and Raiders fan, wore a Knights jersey with his name on the back.

That night, I caught up with the man who led the arena in the singing of the national anthem. He was Keith Dotson, an MGM Resorts festival site worker who told me he was honored and touched to lead the packed arena of 18,000 emotional fans and staff in singing the national anthem.

"I was glad to have my festival team behind me and when the crowd joined in behind me there was an amazing feeling of unity," Dotson said.

It was a night of jumbled emotions as I sat in my seat along the press ledge above the upper bowl and awaited the drop of the puck. I was emotionally spent and the game had not even started. It's hard to find another institution in a town that triggers more emotions than the local sports team.

I have many friends who don't like professional sports, but even they admit that teams unite towns in ways few other institutions can. And this night, Oct. 10, the hockey Gods looked down on T-Mobile Arena. It took only two minutes and 31 seconds into the game for a big, strapping Czech by the name of Tomas Nosek to score the game's first goal for the Golden Knights and the crowd exploded with a cathartic roar.

Then, less than two minutes later, just 4:18 into the game, it was the night's speechmaker, the hometown man, Engelland, with a goal to give the Knights a 2-0 lead.

The Vegas Golden Knights scored early and often during franchise's first-ever regular season home game, defeating the Arizona Coyotes. Photo credit: Daniel Clark

The goals kept coming. This time, it was that man again, Neal, who scored key goals in games one and two, scoring less than two minutes after Engelland's goal. The game was only six minutes and 15 seconds old and the Golden Knights led, 3-0.

Fans were jubilant and the pain of Oct. 1 was temporarily gone. And as if the night was scripted by a grand force from the great beyond, Neal scored again with the game 10 minutes and 42 seconds old. The Golden Knights dropped four goals on the dazed Arizona Coyotes in less than 11 minutes to start the game and fans were hugging and smiling and screaming and it was sheer bedlam.

The Knights gave Las Vegas a 5-2 win to start the home ice legacy. Something was going on in Las Vegas with this hockey team.

31

My second chance in Las Vegas meant returning to bike my old haunts. There was majestic Mount Charleston, where I biked Deer Creek Road at an altitude of more 8,000 feet. It was outside Las Vegas and the peak was just a few feet less of 12,000, with temperatures 20 degrees cooler than those in the Las Vegas Valley.

There was lots of elevation gain. I don't bike fast and I slowly grinded up the mountain to the ski center at the end of Lee Canyon Road. The first time back biking on Mount Charleston was like reuniting with an old pal.

In the fall of 2017, there were also return bike rides in Valley of Fire State Park about an hour north of Las Vegas where rock formations and red colors form a colorful pallet of rock and on the River Mountain Loop Trail in Henderson, Boulder City and Lake Mead National Recreation Area. The River Mountains trail is a 35-mile roller-coaster of a route, snaking its way through rocks and desert terrain with balcony views of Lake Mead.

By late March, the many beavertail cactuses along the River Mountains trail were blooming pink flowers. And these pink flowers made me feel like I was home again. I missed these bursts of pink color dancing atop the green cactuses amid the tan and calico desert landscapes in 2017 because I was stuck in Vero Beach recuperating. But here in the early spring of 2018, my heart soared as I took my first glimpses of these colorful desert splashes.

It was this mash-up of bicycling and nature that connected me to Las Vegas. I know, it's strange that a place known for glitz, neon, bright lights and over-the-top behavior had hooked me with its nature and land. There was no better way to sponge up this connective feeling than via bicycle.

In a world of operators and bullshitters, bicycling is the truth. It requires one thing of you -- willpower. That's the fascinating thing about bicycling. Most people focus on the physical dimension of bicycling. But it's about willpower. There are no words that will propel the bicycle. Riding a bicycle is stunningly fair. You get exactly out of it what you put into it. And here's the best part of all.

You get to your destination using your own human power. There is no motorized propulsion. The motor is in your soul and the fuel comes from your food and your willpower. It simply requires you try your best and you will eventually reach your destination. The bicycle's passenger is also its engine. And that is what is so heartbreaking about motorized vehicles taking out people on bicycles.

Bicyclists first demanded and realized the first paved roads in this country because bicycles pre-dated cars. And now motorists are killing bicyclists and pedestrians. I'm told bicycling is a safe activity. Unfortunately, I can't control the person steering a two-ton missile on four wheels behind me. Which is why the most trusting people in the U.S. are people on bicycles who trust that you the motorist will steer your motorized vehicle around them. Most of the time, you do go around a bicyclist. But sadly, that's not always the case.

32

My 17-year-old Pugsy was dying after I returned to Las Vegas. As much as I knew it was time for her to go, pets have a way of worming their ways into your heart without you knowing it. She was my travel partner from Las Vegas to Vero Beach in March 2016 and from Vero Beach back to Las Vegas in May 2017. She was a gentle creature who could teach quite a few people about manners and respect.

I wrote hundreds of stories with Pugsy resting below my desk and she had become part of the daily rhythm of my life. She was not an athletic dog, but there was a zenmaster quality to her body language that soothed my restless ways. She lived her life with dignity and a hunger for her favorite food -- Grammies' chicken pot pie. I knew the end was near when I broke a story on LVSportsBiz.com in November about the Raiders staging their groundbreaking event on Nov. 13.

Helping me heal and feel back home in Las Vegas. The blooming bea-
vertail cactus in late March 2018.   *Photo credit: Alan Snel*

RIP Pugsy, a beautiful and sweet soul.

I will never forget that date because I had to put Pugsy down the day after -- Nov. 14. The Raiders' groundbreaking had a lot of glitz and flair, as comedian George Lopez hosted the event under the big tent on the stadium site. Everyone from former Raiders greats Howie Long, Jim Plunkett and Tom Flores were there along with Gov. Sandoval and Sisolak, of course.

The truth was my head was in a fog at the groundbreaking because I was dreading the notion of taking the old four-legged girl to the vet the next morning. My good friend, Jean Fajardo, the licensed clinical social worker, was in attendance at the Raiders groundbreaking and she was a gem that night giving me emotional support.

Journeys of healing don't have to be alone. There are people in your lives who care and who will listen and who will offer a hand. You're not alone. Emotional recovery is not easy. But be willing to ask for help and receive help. Sometimes guys want to tough it out. But being stoic doesn't necessarily help the healing. Trauma makes us vulnerable -- physically and emotionally.

So, let people help.

33

LVSportsBiz.com was picking up steam as 2017 turned to 2018. I was reporting on UNLV sports trying to create a new branding personality with a new athletic director, Desiree Reed-Francois, at the helm. The folks at UFC were working on a new media rights deal with ESPN and its various platforms. The owners of the Triple A baseball team in Las Vegas, Howard Hughes Corporation, had celebrated an $80 million ballpark naming rights windfall from the Las Vegas Convention and Visitors Authority tourism agency to help build its $150 million Pacific Coast League ballyard next to the Golden Knights' training center is suburban Summerlin 15 miles west of the Strip.

The new Las Vegas Aces WNBA team was launching its product with a short runway for liftoff to sell tickets, sponsorships and marketing deals.

*Las Vegas Aces All-Star and WNBA Rookie of the Year
A'ja Wilson during the Aces' inaugural season in Las Vegas.
Photo credit: J. Tyge O'Donnell*

*Esports became big business in Las Vegas in 2018.
Photo credit: Daniel Clark*

The also new Las Vegas Lights FC soccer team was putting together its roster of new players for preseason games in February 2018, with an owner ready to release a bunch of zany sponsorship deals in his bag of tricks.

The folks down at Las Vegas Motor Speedway were busy planning to stage NASCAR weekends in March and September for the first time ever in the track's history, with South Point hotel-casino signing a deal to be the title sponsor for the venue's second big NASCAR race.

Then, I was surprised to learn that playing video games could bring big money for the best players in a new entertainment category called esports in Las Vegas.

Millennials wearing video game-playing jerseys were descending on Las Vegas, which was emerging as a co-hub with Los Angeles as the center for the esports craze. MGM Resorts International had converted a club in the Luxor hotel-casino into an esports arena and a Caesars Entertainment property off the Strip also hosted battle royale-style esports gamer leagues.

So even though the Vegas Golden Knights and the Raiders stadium development were the two flashpoint subjects for LVSportsBiz.com, there were plenty of other sports-business news to cover.

My first LVSportsBiz.com road trip came in December 2017, when I followed Interstate 15 to Southern California to report on back-to-back Golden Knights games in Anaheim and Los Angeles. It would be the first time I visited the Ducks' home ice, while the following night's game at Staples Center in downtown Los Angeles allowed me to catch up with Michael Roth, the PR chief for Anschutz Entertainment Group, which owned the Kings and the arena.

In another example of bicycling intersecting with LVSportsBiz.com, I had covered AEG's Tour of California bike race a few years earlier and Roth knew of my love for bicycling. I had a cool story lined up on how AEG also owned a piece of the Golden Knights' arena in Las Vegas, making the Kings-owning AEG partners with Golden Knights owner Bill Foley, who also owned a piece of T-Mobile Arena.

The Los Angeles field trip also gave me the chance to see my nephew, Sam Kalra, who was in his first year at Bank of America and he would be my cameraman when I interviewed AEG's Chief Executive Officer Dan Beckerman between periods of the Golden Knights-Kings game.

It was special to hang with Sam along press row, as I processed the video of the interview and wrote the story on the unusual business relationship between the Kings and the Golden Knights, teams that were foes on the ice yet business partners off it because of their co-ownership of T-Mobile Arena.

It was another enterprise story no other news source had and it came together because of my sources in the industry and my sense of reporting news beyond the press release.

The news business is a pure exercise of love for most reporters. The money that newspaper reporters earn is modest at best.

I was generating enough ad revenue at LVSportsBiz.com to pay the bills.

But here's the most important part -- I was in charge of my life and setting my own time schedule.

As I was getting older, I realized that time was my most precious and valuable commodity and I was in charge of spending it the way that my life needed to balance LVSportsBiz.com with bicycling with those I loved.

Which brings me to the world of newspapers, a career that took me from metro New York City to South Florida and Tampa Bay to Denver and Seattle and now finally to Las Vegas.

Newspapers -- specifically newsrooms -- are like no other business. News people are not business people. We chase stories, are clueless about the cost of purveying news and live for the high of presenting information or a look at life never considered before.

When reporting a story, it's a world of nuance and art and a million shades of gray, not formulas and templates because writing news like a robot doing a mathematical equation will get your news organization irrelevant very fast.

The news business is also a grueling grind, a regiment that typically doesn't fit the ebb and flow of a person's life. And that's why publishing LVSportsBiz.com was ideal for not only getting over the crash but also for giving me a platform to recover my joy of writing and reporting again after my Vero Beach 32963 experience.

I learned the Las Vegas Review-Journal had eliminated my old business of sports reporting position in its newsroom. So, I was able to resurrect my old beat without competition from a reporter designated to cover this area of news. And I have been able to carve out a news niche that has more than 525 stories during the website's first 16 months with more than 130,000 readers.

I don't mind LVSportsBiz.com taking on the field in Las Vegas. It's been terrific flying solo, surveying a news landscape and guided by my own instincts. But the truth is that I have had news mates with me at LVSportsBiz.com -- talented photographer Daniel Clark, who received the only roaming photographer credential at the Stanley Cup Finals from the National Hockey League so that he was able to document the amazing emotional scenes off the ice.

Clark's photos added so much to LVSportsBiz.com's stories.

I first met Clark when he was a freelance photographer at the Review-Journal, and I was impressed with his talent and can-do attitude.

When I started reporting stories for LVSportsBiz.com, I knew top-notch photos were a must. I also needed a photographer who was news savvy enough to understand that these were not sports stories, that the stories were about the mash-up of business, commerce, politics and consumer issues behind the sports developments, teams and stadiums in Las Vegas.

Clark's first assignment was a union pep rally and picnic to celebrate the Raiders stadium at a North Las Vegas park in the heat of a Sunday summer day in 2017.

He captured Steve Sisolak working the Laborers 872 union crowd and the union's leader, Tommy White, exhorting the union faithful to get behind the Raiders. The local union even had a bus decorated in the Raiders' silver and black colors -- images caught perfectly by Clark.

Photo credit: Daniel Clark

Photo credit: Daniel Clark

Laborers Local 872 leader Tommy Whites addresses 872 members at Raiders stadium rally picnic in summer of 2017.
Photo credit: Daniel Clark

Clark County Commission Chairman and Raiders stadium supporter Steve Sisolak, who is running for governor.
Photo credit: Daniel Clark

Raiders President Marc Badain at a stadium board meeting in early 2018.   Photo credit: Daniel Clark

A NHL ref at a Vegas Golden Knights-Los Angeles Kings playoff game at Staples Center in downtown Los Angeles in April 2018. Photo credit: Erik John Ricardo

His work was exceptional, whether it was documenting Raiders President Marc Badain taking in the action at stadium authority meetings or fans buying hats at the 51s' home-opener or Raiders owner Mark Davis swapping stories with fans at Las Vegas Aces games.

But Clark shined at the Stanley Cup Finals at T-Mobile Arena. He hustled his ass off to take stunning pictures of fans, vendors and even the famed Stanley Cup trophy itself as he sent me photos in waves. I then updated LVSportsBiz.com with Clark's work throughout the home games as the Golden Knights hosted the Washington Capitals in Games 1, 2 and 5.

Clark was not the only photographer who took photos for LVSportsBiz.com. In September 2017, I was bicycling along the Red Rock loop when I met a bicyclist with pannier bags packed with bottles of water. Erik Ricardo was carrying the extra weight on his road bicycle to train for a bike tour along the Oregon coast. What better way to prep for those roller-coaster hills along the Pacific Coast Highway in Oregon than to pedal the steep hills of the Red Rock loop with 20 pounds of water bottles?

We chatted and I learned Erik was a photographer, with a specialty in portraits and he soon became a member of the LVSportsBiz.com photo staff.

Ricardo's work was stellar, from covering UNLV football games to Golden Knights games in Los Angeles during the playoffs to a gorgeous portrait of Golden Knights founding partner Joe Maloof in front of T-Mobile Arena. (Arena security tried to shoo us away and it didn't seem to matter to security that a co-owner of the Golden Knights was the photo subject. I called an MGM Resorts International PR guy and he vouched for LVSportsBiz.com to security and we got the photo.)

LVSportsBiz.com did not have a big budget. But we had lots of persistence. And other terrific photographers, like veteran newsman L.E. Baskow and J. Tyge O'Donnell, the son of a former White House photographer who was dispatched by the military to chronicle the bombings of Japan during World War 11 in 1945.

34

It was Jan. 21, 2018 and the Vegas Golden Knights defeated the Carolina Hurricanes, 5-1, to take over first place in the NHL with the most points in the league.

Weeks later, the Golden Knights first clinched a position in the playoffs and then the Pacific Division title with a win over division rival San Jose thanks to a short-handed, between-the-legs shot-of-the-year by emerging star William Karlsson.

Along the way, the Golden Knights were striking gold off the ice as well. Golden Knights home games had evolved into what I called "sportstainment" events, where the home team was racking up wins while Cirque du Soleil performers were contorting their bodies in between periods.

On the day after Valentine's Day in February, the team took love to new heights when a couple became engaged between periods one and two and then were married during a ceremony officiated by Elvis between periods two and three.

"She had no clue I was going to do it. I took a risk. We knew we were supposed to be together," a proud freshly-married Steve Poscente told me after the game. The newlyweds received matching Golden Knights jerseys with "Mr. and Mrs. Poscente" on the back for each.

The team's marketing chief, Brian Killingsworth, said having both an engagement and a wedding at the same sports event made history. "We think this might be the first time a team has had a proposal and wedding in the same game. But this is Vegas and part of the mystique of the city," Killingsworth said.

During Knights coach Gerard Gallant's post-game press conference, I asked the coach if he would mind if one of his players got married during the game. In the position to crack a joke, Gallant explained he could live with a player tying the knot between periods as long as he was not playing during the game.

Gallant then cracked a smile at the Knights PR chief, Eric Tosi, who gave the coach known as Turk a thumb's up. Sports reporters enjoyed the joke during the coach's post-game press session that typically involves hockey strategy talk. "That's Vegas. That's what they like here," Gallant said.

Even star forward William Karlsson couldn't help watch the wedding ceremony in between periods two and three. "It was pretty cool. I looked at the Jumbotron and smiled during the wedding," Karlsson told me at his locker after the game.

If you think the Golden Knights are good at love, the team went one step further. Try finding homes for 164 abandoned pomeranian puppies, left in a U-Haul truck without food and water off a highway in Nevada near the California border. A week before Christmas, the team worked with the Animal Foundation to kick off the adoption process at the Golden Knights' training center.

Literally hundreds of Pomeranian lovers came to City National Arena for an auction for five of the dogs and to submit $200 entries in a contest for another 10 of the Poms. It was the team that contacted the Animal Foundation about helping the abandoned pups find new homes.

"The team came to us and their objective is to raise awareness about the journey of these dogs," Daniel Neel, Animal Foundation chief finance and development officer, told me that day. "We did expect the interest to be huge. We've had thousands of inquiries."

35

The Golden Knights rolled into the playoffs as division champs and rolled through the playoffs to the Stanley Cup Finals. During the playoffs, I hopped on my fat-tire Surly Pugsley model bike and pedaled a mile to the training center, which was packed with fans.

You know all about the Golden Knights season. It was Miracle on Ice meets Elvis meets Disney meets Blue Man Group meets 1969 Miracle Mets. Out of this could-never-be-scripted inaugural season blossomed a Fleury statue made of chocolate at the Bellagio; Lady Liberty wearing a 620-pound VGK jersey at Tropicana Avenue and the Strip; and a giant puck stuck into an elevator tower of a pedestrian bridge.

The Golden Knights' season also fostered a fun collection of fan characters who became mini-celebrities. There was the Knights' most recognizable fan, a retired 24-year Air Force veteran who looked like the Wolverine superhero. Jason Griego, with his Marvel Comics character look, was featured on the T-Mobile Arena's center hung scoreboard just about every game.

Replica of Lady Liberty wearing a Golden Knights jersey in front of New York-New York hotel-casino on the Strip.   Photo credit: L.E. Baskow

*Super fan Jason Griego, AKA "the Wolverine"
Photo credit: J. Tyge O'Donnell*

Then, there was a Jack Russell terrier named Bark-Andre Furry, owned by Rick Williams, who showed up with Bark-Andre at every practice and was featured everywhere from the NHL Awards Show red carpet to a Golden Knights credit card sponsorship deal with Credit One Bank.

Drawing NHL air time was also Logan "The Girl With The Hat" Sokoloski, a 10-year-old at the time who became enamored with the Golden Knights after the team beat the Colorado Avalanche, 7-0, on Nevada Day Oct. 27, 2017. It was the Golden Knights' star goalie, Fleury, who gave the pint-sized fan her "The Girl With The Hat" nickname.

The Golden Knights' unparalleled success for a first-year major league team spawned a whole subculture of these fan personalities and helped soothe the emotional pain that engulfed Las Vegas Oct. 1.

The Golden Knights' season ended June 7, when the Washington Capitals raised the Stanley Cup after Game 5 at T-Mobile Arena. The Capitals defeated the Golden Knights, 4-3, after the home team held a 3-2 lead in the third period.

The weird thing was that Golden Knights fans were disappointed, but not necessarily devastated. They relished the historic miracle season with the "welcome to impossible" slogan that marked the wild ride to the Stanley Cup Finals.

June 7, 2018 was also important for me for another reason. The date marked one year of publishing LVSportsBiz.com. And I also was healing, too.

The Stanley Cup.   Photo credit: Daniel Clark

36

On March 7, 2017, I set off for a morning bike ride in Vero Beach, Florida that turned my life upside-down. I came face-to-face with my mortality, surviving a near-fatal crash that I don't even remember and never heard from the motorist who nearly killed me on my daily ride.

Then on June 1, 2017, less than three months later, I set off for another bike ride from a central Las Vegas house that was 2,500 miles away from Vero Beach. On this June 2017 day, I woke up in Las Vegas for the first time since leaving in late February 2016 and I was committed to riding a bicycle to the overlook on the Red Rock scenic drive at 4,771 feet.

The day's first light came around 5 a.m. I was excited. After feeding Pugsy and taking her out in the backyard, I dressed for my first bicycle ride back in Las Vegas. I was so eager to return to my old daily haunt -- that Red Rock Canyon scenic loop, where the early-morning ride is as much meditative as it is physical.

I biked six miles west from central Las Vegas to the western suburbs of Summerlin, the gateway to Red Rock Canyon. It's a bike ride that's all uphill to the Red Rock loop, that 13-mile U.S. Bureau of Land Management-operated strip of pavement that meanders its way into the Spring Mountains foothills at Red Rock Canyon.

During all those days when I was recovering back in Vero Beach in March and April I vowed to myself that on the first morning back in Las Vegas, if I was strong enough and healed enough, I would return to the Red Rock loop overlook 86 days after being knocked out by a distracted motorist on the other side of the country.

The house I was watching at the time is probably around 2,400 feet or so and I was obsessed with making it back to the start of Red Rock loop entrance, which is about 3,600 feet and then the overlook at 4,771 feet.

As I turned right off of state road 159 and entered the loop road, it felt great to be back. To think, I gave this up under my own free will 16 months earlier. It's about 4 1/2 miles of climbing to reach the overlook. But this was one ride where I didn't mind the challenging upward grade.

I couldn't believe I was doing this. I was biking on a road I thought I'd never see again when I was lying in a hospital ICU in Fort Pierce less than three months earlier.

It's mostly all uphill and a grind -- but I never enjoyed an uphill bike ride more than this road that offered a perch to see a red rock ridge, then a white sandstone hiking area and finally a high tan-colored desert terrain dotted by green, spiky vegetation with needles that are razor sharp.

I biked higher and higher and higher. I took a break to snap a selfie while wearing a back-up bike helmet that replaced the one that saved me back in March. When I reached the top and pulled into the overlook parking lot, it was emotional.

I took off my helmet, peered at the sloping land before me and sobbed. I can't think of another time when I was so happy to be alive. My criteria for happiness had changed because of a motorist who smashed his car into me less than three months earlier.

Soaking up the Red Rock views at 4,771 feet above sea level and filling my lungs with air was enough to make me happy. LVSportsBiz.com gave my mental senses a purpose. I was home in Red Rock and in Las Vegas.

37

This book's message is simple. If I can overcome a trauma, you can, too. But it's not going to be easy. Overcoming trauma is hard. In fact, I can understand how it can be easy to get emotionally stuck and not move forward.

I was so happy to return to Las Vegas and Red Rock Canyon and create my own job here that gives me a daily purpose. But I still retain a small simmering level of anger and bitterness over the fact that the motorist who drove his car into me was never held accountable by police and that he probably should not have been operating a motorized vehicle in the first place.

The crash is always with me -- physically, speaking. There's a sticky feeling below the skin above my knee joint and there's a slight puffiness to the skin around my knee that will never go away. My lower back seizes when I stand in place for more than a few minutes. And I came away not as physically nimble as I was before.

But the crash forced me to re-evaluate my life. Faced with mortality, decisions become easier to make because the mental clutter falls away. It became easier to make priorities, including writing this book to share what I have learned about healing, recovery, purpose and affirmation. Here are my suggestions.

The first thing I did was identify a new goal -- return to Las Vegas and start LVSportsBiz.com. It gave a purpose and structure to my life that allowed me to look ahead and put the crash behind me. The new site tapped into a dynamic and growing industry in Las Vegas, where new teams were being launched and new sports venues were being built.

The content for LVSportsBiz.com required a mash-up of journalistic skills that I had acquired over a lifetime -- reporting on a variety of disciplines such as local government, business, economic development, politics and consumer (fan) issues; writing in several different styles that ranged from conversational to hard-hitting; and providing images from talented photographers who understand that the LVSportsBiz.com was all about the action behind the scenes and off the field.

The timing of the historic Golden Knights' season provided so many stories to report on and write about that it created a core of content for LVSportsBiz.com. In fact, the deep pool of stories from the Raiders stadium to the new teams in Las Vegas to the slate of major sports events in the market required so much of a journalistic time commitment that it limited the time I spent reflecting back on the crash that could have ended my life in March 2017.

The second thing is making sure that the purpose -- in my case, starting LVSportsBiz.com -- was an organic move and not forced. I have a career in covering the business side of sports in several markets around the country, including right here in Las Vegas, and I even started a national site on the topic for FOXSports.com, so I had a feel for the logistical demands and requirements for a site of this nature.

And the timing could not have been more perfect. I caught the wave of this expanding industry and I'm riding it through the opening of the Raiders stadium in July 2020 and the start of an NBA team that I predict will come a few years after the Raiders move here. While identifying a purpose is essential to move beyond the trauma, it's important to not blindly become a workaholic to avoid confronting the deep emotions that accompany a trauma. I acknowledge that my frenetic pace of writing stories for the first year of LVSportsBiz.com was a way of avoiding the trauma's emotional pain -- which is a universal way of dealing and coping with trauma. But it doesn't work in the long run. This is another reason why I wrote this book -- to confront, relive and process what happened in a safe and emotionally thoughtful way that I had control over. It's about the pursuit of realizing a purpose, while also confronting and processing the pain. As my sister, Deborah, put it, if you don't deal with the trauma, the trauma will deal with you.

The third thing is to take any anger or bitterness and re-purpose it into motivation to build your goal. It's hard to move forward when you feel justice was not realized in your trauma. But harboring anger for a motorist who got away with nearly killing me means he would continue to hurt me. Brophy never apologized or reached out to me before he died. A grudge hurts the person who holds it more than the targeted person of that grudge. Without a grudge, it's easier to move forward. I like the words, "move forward," instead of "move on" or "get over it." That's because I won't ever get over the memory of this trauma because when I hear news of bicyclist fatalities, it reactivates the emotions related to the crash. But I certainly can move forward.

The fourth thing is to avoid thinking about the "what ifs" surrounding a trauma. What if I quit the Las Vegas Review-Journal, never even moved to Vero Beach and just started LVSportsBiz.com while I still lived in Las Vegas? What if the Escape Adventures bicycle touring business in Florida worked out and I had a bike tour to lead on March 7, 2017? What if I started my bike ride an hour later that day? The what ifs don't accomplish much and serve as wasted energy.

And finally the fifth thing -- especially for men -- is to acknowledge the physical and emotional pain and be willing to accept help. Guys sometimes want to be stoic and gut out a trauma and they don't realize they could be acting out in ways to cope with a trauma when people can provide help all along.

In my case, my dear sister, Deborah, provided a road map to understand how to navigate the emotions that pile up amid overcoming a trauma. My friend Jean also provided a helpful ear as I recovered in Vero Beach before I returned to Las Vegas.

I realized that discussing the role of bicycling, the launch of LVSportsBiz.com, the Golden Knights' magical first season and the intense growth of the Las Vegas sports market provided me with the vehicle for this passage of healing and recovery.

There's enough emotional distance to say I'm in a good place now. Remember, it's all about balance. In my case, it was the dedication and commitment to launching and sustaining LVSportsBiz.com, while also taking days off to ride a bicycle to soak up and appreciate our awe-inspiring natural world. Two weeks ago in late September 2018, I bicycled a road along the Grand Canyon and my heart soared when I stopped to look at this vast opening in the earth. It was the first time I saw this natural wonder since returning to Las Vegas in late May 2017.

The sun was setting and the light was perfect. I felt complete again.

**